THE UPPER ROOM

WHERE THE WORLD MEETS TO PRAY

Susan Hibbins
UK editor

INTERDENOMINATIONAL
INTERNATIONAL
INTERRACIAL

Mul

CW00606472

The Bible Reading Fellowship
15 The Chambers, Vineyard
Abingdon OX14 3FE
brf.org.uk
biblereadingnotes.org.uk

The Bible Reading Fellowship (BRF) is a Registered Charity (233280)

ISBN 978 0 85746 447 7

The Upper Room © BRF 2017

Cover image © Thinkstock
Map on page 6 © Thinkstock

Acknowledgements
The New Revised Standard Version of the Bible, Anglicised Edition, copyright © 1989,
1995 by the Division of Christian Education of the National Council of the Churches of
Christ in the USA. Used by permission. All rights reserved.

Scripture quotations taken from The Holy Bible, New International Version (Anglicised
edition) copyright © 1979, 1984, 2011 by Biblica. Used by permission of Hodder
& Stoughton Publishers, an Hachette UK company. All rights reserved. 'NIV' is a
registered trademark of Biblica. UK trademark number 1448790.

Extracts from the Authorised Version of the Bible (The King James Bible), the rights in
which are vested in the Crown, are reproduced by permission of the Crown's Patentee,
Cambridge University Press.

Extracts from CEB copyright © 2011 by Common English Bible.

Printed by Gutenberg Press, Tarxien, Malta

How to use *The Upper Room*

The Upper Room is ideal in helping us spend a quiet time with God each day. Each daily entry is based on a passage of scripture, and is followed by a meditation and prayer. Each person who contributes a meditation to the magazine seeks to relate their experience of God in a way that will help those who use *The Upper Room* every day.

Here are some guidelines to help you make best use of *The Upper Room*:

1. Read the passage of Scripture. It is a good idea to read it more than once, in order to have a fuller understanding of what it is about and what you can learn from it.
2. Read the meditation. How does it relate to your own experience? Can you identify with what the writer has outlined from their own experience or understanding?
3. Pray the written prayer. Think about how you can use it to relate to people you know, or situations that need your prayers today.
4. Think about the contributor who has written the meditation. Some *Upper Room* users include this person in their prayers for the day.
5. Meditate on the 'Thought for the day' and the 'Prayer Focus', perhaps using them again as the focus for prayer or direction for action.

Why is it important to have a daily quiet time? Many people will agree that it is the best way of keeping in touch every day with the God who sustains us, and who sends us out to do his will and show his love to the people we encounter each day. Meeting with God in this way reassures us of his presence with us, helps us to discern his will for us and makes us part of his worldwide family of Christian people through our prayers.

I hope that you will be encouraged as you use the magazine regularly as part of your daily devotions, and that God will richly bless you as you read his word and seek to learn more about him.

Susan Hibbins
UK Editor

In times of/For help with . . .

Below is a list of entries in this copy of *The Upper Room* relating to situations or emotions with which we may need help:

Inspired to forgive

'Bear with one another and, if anyone has a complaint against another, forgive each other; just as the Lord has forgiven you, so you also must forgive' (Colossians 3:13, NRSV).

I remember the first time I visited a women's prison. Members of a local congregation in Salta, Argentina, went to this prison regularly, and they invited me to join them as the celebrant for a Communion service with the women. The prison was unlike those I was familiar with in the United States. This one was more like a large house with guards and security at the entrance. The women mixed together freely, washing their clothes and hanging them in the yard to dry, raising their children, and helping one another with other daily chores. It was almost as if they were a family—guards and inmates alike. As with any family, strong emotions often arose among them. If you were getting along with the other inmates and the guards, life was good; if you weren't, life could be miserable.

After celebrating Communion, an inmate named Ana told me about a particular meditation from *El Aposento Alto*, the Spanish edition of *The Upper Room*, which had affected her. The meditation described how the guards in a men's prison asked a minister to hold a Communion service for both the guards and the inmates. The guards said that they wanted to overcome any animosity that either they or the inmates had for each other. The story inspired Ana, and it led her to forgive one of her guards and build a friendship with her. Ana asked me if I would sign a copy of *El Aposento Alto* as a gift to the guard.

Thinking about my conversation with Ana, I realised that this is what Communion is about: forgiveness, renewal and love. For me, this story represents the power of *The Upper Room*: Christians across the world learning from one another and supporting each other in their journeys of faith. My prayer is that each of us will find in the pages of this magazine the encouragement to forgive and to love as Ana did.

Carmen Gaud
Former Editor, El Aposento Alto

Where the world meets to pray

Pakistan: Since 1952, *The Upper Room* has been translated into Urdu, the national language of Pakistan.

India: In Odisha, churches and schools use *The Upper Room* during daily quiet time. The magazine 'inspires young people to have Christ-centred lives,' says Manasi Mohanty, the Odia edition's editor.

Sri Lanka: The publishing team in Sri Lanka hopes to lead devotional writing workshops to encourage readers to share their faith stories.

Susan Hibbins writes...

Recently my daily Bible reading was the story of the feeding of the five thousand in John 6:1–13. I thought back to my Sunday school days, when this was a familiar passage, and we were encouraged to be like the boy who brought all that he had and gave it to Jesus.

There are a number of interpretations of what actually happened that day: Jesus literally turned the small amount of food into enough to feed the multitude of people who had come to hear him; or, when people saw the boy's example, they followed it and began to share what they had with their neighbours, so that all were fed, being two examples.

What struck me when reading this story again was the comments of the disciples, and what Jesus was trying to teach them—and us—through what happened that day. Jesus, seeing the crowd arriving, asked them, 'Where shall we buy bread for these people to eat?' Reasonably enough perhaps, Philip replies that it would cost an enormous amount of money to buy sufficient bread for the crowd to have even a small amount each. Now is the moment that Andrew brings forward the boy who has 'five small barley loaves and two small fish', but, says Andrew, 'how far will they go among so many?' But in Jesus' hands, the food becomes more than enough for everyone to share, and there is plenty left over.

Are we like the disciples that day? We may feel we have little to offer to Jesus, or we look at other people and feel that they have much more in the way of ability or talent, compared to ourselves. How can we make a difference in our church life, or in our walk of discipleship? How can we, with our meagre resources, help even those around us, let alone those in the wider world?

The truth is that if we bring whatever we have to Jesus, whether it is a tangible material gift, or our own time, talent or other ability, he can use and multiply it beyond anything we can imagine. Two small fish and five small bread rolls became enough to feed a huge crowd: what could he do in the world today with what each of us can give to him?

Susan Hibbins
Editor of the UK edition

The Bible readings are selected with great care, and we urge you to include the suggested reading in your devotional time.

Family Faith

Read Proverbs 3:3–6
Trust in the Lord with all your heart.
Proverbs 3:5 (NIV)

I became the first Christian in my family and the joy I found in Jesus Christ led me to speak the good news. But I was rejected by my own family. My sister did not want me to practise my Christian faith in our shared bedroom—no Bible, no prayer, no Christian radio, no praise. My heart was broken, and I cried out to God, 'Lord, I have been praying for my family to know you, but now I have nowhere to pray.'

I heard a small voice telling me, 'Seon, why do you think you have nowhere to pray? Pray in the bathroom.' I was surprised, but this message from God brought comfort to my broken heart.

We had two bathrooms in our house. I asked my family to use the bathroom next to the living room while I prayed in the other one from midnight to 1 am. The first night I sat on the edge of the bath and burst into tears. But as I read the Bible and prayed, God's peace and grace surrounded me. God turned my sorrow into joy.

That's how my 'bathroom years' began; every night, I felt as if I were going to the seashore to meet my Lord Jesus. By God's grace, my parents and sister later became Christians. Sometimes when I have a problem or need a deep conversation with God, I still pray in the bathroom, trusting that God will meet me there.

Prayer: *Dear God, bless our hearts to trust you and your word, so that we keep praying for our loved ones who are not Christian. Amen*

Thought for the day: To whom can I speak good news today?

Young Seon Kim (Tanzania)

Every Believer's Call

Read Galatians 6:1–6

Like living stones, let yourselves be built into a spiritual house, to be a holy priesthood, to offer spiritual sacrifices acceptable to God through Jesus Christ.
1 Peter 2:5 (NRSV)

As an Upper Room staff member who is blind, I have shared laughter and tears with our Braille readers. While I initially contacted them about subscriptions, together we have found an unbreakable bond in Christ Jesus. These conversations reminded me that we are called to be a holy priesthood in Jesus Christ. But what does that mean?

As priest of Israel, Aaron interceded for the people—demonstrated by the breastplate he wore: 'Aaron shall bear the names of the children of Israel in the breastplate of judgment upon his heart' (Exodus 28:29, KJV). Aaron carried the children of Israel upon his heart as he prayed and offered sacrifices for them.

We are called to do the same for one another, following Paul's exhortation to bear one another's burdens in Christ. In this way we fulfil that call to be priests, living stones and spiritual houses. While talking with my fellow readers of the Braille edition of *The Upper Room*, it would have been easy to say, 'That's not my concern.' But how could I hear their joys and sorrows without bearing their burdens with them? Such is the call to every believer in Christ. He bore on the cross the burden of humanity's sin so that we can all live abundant lives as forgiven people.

Prayer: *Lord Jesus, soften our hearts to those around us and help us to show them your love. Amen*

Thought for the day: We can imitate Christ by helping to bear one another's burdens.

Brooke Pernice (Tennessee, US)

The Wind at Your Back

Read Revelation 21:1–7

Your sun shall no more go down, or your moon withdraw itself; for the Lord will be your everlasting light, and your days of mourning shall be ended.
Isaiah 60:20 (NRSV)

I once told someone about my struggles with a habitual sin. I asked for advice and support. The response was 'Well, if you're a Christian, you shouldn't have any trouble controlling your demons.'

I wanted to scream: 'That's not helpful, nor is it true!' We are Christians because we have accepted that we are sinful and need God's guidance. Later, I asked God to forgive me for this habitual sin. But even though I knew that God had forgiven me, I continued to be overwhelmed by shame and guilt.

One Sunday, my pastor preached on God's limitless grace: 'Sin will always be with us,' she said, 'but we need to confess our wrongdoings to the Lord and to move on. Forget about it. After all, doesn't God forget about it?' Her words lifted my spirits. She was absolutely right. But I still struggle to let go of the past and focus on improving in the future.

A family member once told me, 'God is the wind at your back, not the rain in your face.' God doesn't hold us back, constantly reminding us of our sin. He guides us forward. We may be the rain in our own faces. If we continue to forgive ourselves and move beyond our past sins, we can accept God's new covenant and start fresh.

Prayer: *Dear God, forgive us. Help us to accept your forgiveness and leave the burden of sin behind. Amen*

Thought for the day: God forgives my sins: I can forgive myself.

Nathaniel T. McMaster (Washington, DC, US)

Created for a Purpose

Read Jeremiah 29:11–13

I know the plans I have for you, says the Lord, plans for your welfare and not for harm, to give you a future with hope.
Jeremiah 29:11 (NRSV)

I am only four feet seven inches tall. At school, I was constantly teased about my height. The ugly words troubled me. One day I asked God, 'Why did you make me so small?'

Now I am a special education teacher who specialises in teaching pupils with impaired vision. Early in my work as a specialist, the school wanted to place a pupil who was blind into a pre-school class with sighted children. I would assist him as the teacher gave instruction to the whole class. This had never been done before.

On his first day of lessons I led Carlos into the room and sat beside him. As the teacher greeted the class I whispered to him, 'I'm right here.' A spiritual insight surged through me. God was saying, 'For this purpose I created you.'

Being small was perfect: I fitted into the pupils' tiny chairs and was able to sit by their desks. I taught Carlos to read Braille and helped him achieve success in grade after grade until he left high school. With God's help, I was able to teach students with special needs for 20 years. I am thankful that the Lord used me, all four feet seven inches, to help so many people.

Prayer: *Dear Lord, help us to trust your design. Thank you for helping us to persevere. Amen*

Thought for the day: God has a purpose for me.

Marion Young (Texas, US)

Kindling

Read Matthew 4:12–17

[Jesus said] 'I have come to bring fire on the earth, and how I wish it were already kindled!'
Luke 12:49 (NIV)

In more recent years we have been blessed with central heating in the house. It responds to our need for warmth with just the press of a switch. It wasn't always like that—as I recalled on holiday when we stayed in a remote rural cottage. I found myself once again kneeling in front of a long-dead fire, brushing ashes out of the grate before relaying kindling wood and small coal ready to be relit in the evening.

Although it may have seemed a daily chore in past years, cleaning out the grate was a useful morning exercise with a spiritual meaning: there can be no new fire without first cleaning out the old ashes.

I sometimes long for greater enthusiasm among people of faith—and in myself—and I am challenged by the words of Jesus as he longed for his 'kingdom fire' to be lit in the whole world. From the very beginning of his ministry Jesus taught that repentance and moving on from the past is the key to rekindling our trust in God. A deeper spiritual life and gospel enthusiasm follow a cleaning out of old things—the old me—ready for a Spirit-spark.

I think I miss that morning fire-lighting, and its daily spiritual challenge!

Prayer: *Lord, clean me out. Relight the fire of your love in me. Amen*

Thought for the day: Each new day we can be rekindled by God's grace.

Colin Harbach (Cumbria, England)

The Question

Read 2 Corinthians 11:16–33

I am not saying this because I am in need, for I have learned to be content whatever the circumstances.
Philippians 4:11 (NIV)

After my first few months working overseas—struggling with learning a new language and experiencing a culture very different from my own—I was beginning to have a negative attitude. Then the Holy Spirit brought to my mind my last training session for this work. I looked up the verse quoted above and remembered the question our mentor asked us after reading Philippians 4: 'Have you really learned to trust the Lord and be content in all circumstances?'

Paul's words encouraged me but were also convicting. He experienced persecution, imprisonment and other trials; yet he learned to be content. I realised that, in comparison, my troubles were very small. I prayed, and the Lord restored my trust that he would help me to be content whatever challenges I encounter.

When we pray about our struggles and seek God's help, we become newly aware of his power in our lives. The same power that raised Jesus from the grave can transform us, giving us joyful hearts and grateful spirits no matter what comes our way.

Prayer: *Dear God, help us to trust you and be content, knowing that your deep love for us will see us through. Amen*

Thought for the day: I can overcome difficulties with God's help.

Karol Ruth Whaley (California, US)

PRAYER FOCUS: SOMEONE MOVING TO A NEW COUNTRY

Learning to Listen

Read Mark 4:21–25

Jesus said, 'Very truly I tell you, whoever hears my word and believes him who sent me has eternal life.'
John 5:24 (NIV)

My husband and I have been birdwatching together for 20 years. Recognising bird songs helps us to know which bird is near so that we can more easily spot it. At first I only recognised a few songs, but now I know the songs of all the birds in our area.

One spring morning, my husband and I paused on our walk through the woods to listen for more birds. The symphony of birdsong that morning reminded me of Jesus' words in today's reading: 'Consider carefully what you hear…' (Mark 4:24). I paused to think: have I been as attentive to words from God as I should be? Do I focus as carefully on God as I did to learn each individual bird song?

Paying careful attention to scripture, sermons and God's whispers in our hearts helps us grow in faith. If we devote all our attention to careful listening, as I did when learning bird songs, we can increase our understanding and insight. But if we fail to pay attention, we may lose our perception of Christ and God's kingdom. We can make a commitment to listen for God with eagerness and attentiveness so that we may deepen our faith.

Prayer: *Dear Lord, please help us to be attentive to you so that we may grow in faith and in our knowledge of you. Amen*

Thought for the day: How can I pay more attention to God today?

Eugenie Daniels (Massachusetts, US)

Using Time Wisely

Read Ephesians 5:1–20

Be careful then how you live, not as unwise people but as wise, making the most of the time, because the days are evil.
Ephesians 5:15–16 (NRSV)

One night, after a period of feeling detached from God, I received word that one of my childhood friends had died in a tragic traffic accident. The news was so painful that I felt as if I had died inside, but it also caused me to reflect on my life in an extraordinary way and turn back to God. The worst pain of all was wondering why it had taken such a tragic event to make me reflect on my life and seek God again. As with many of the mysteries in this life, I still do not have an answer. The only thing I know with certainty is that I don't want to be detached anymore from the one who gave me life, from the Lord of hosts, from my loving Father.

Many of us can be ambitious about our finances, social position and recognition, but sometimes we forget that the Lord has given us these lives we cherish. When I find myself striving for success I have to ask myself: am I putting my time to good use? Am I really living as if this were my last day? These and other questions help to transform my thinking. God, who is rich in mercy, gives us opportunities again and again to repent of our wrongdoings and foolishness. When we do so, we can feel reborn.

Prayer: *Dear God, remind us that you are the one who gives us life. And help us to cherish each day. Amen*

Thought for the day: Each day of life is a sacred gift from God.

Wendy Orellana (Barquisimeto, Venezuela)

Clean Viewing

Read Matthew 23:23–26

Rid yourselves of all the offences you have committed, and get a new heart and a new spirit.
Ezekiel 18:31 (NIV)

Winter seemed to drag on for months and left all the windows of our home covered with a dull film. On the first nice day of spring, my wife washed them. She went from one to the next, scrubbing and cleaning. Later, as we looked out of a window together, she said, 'How bright and new the world looks through clean windows!'

This experience reminded me of how my perspective changed when I first accepted Christ. Suddenly everything and everyone seemed sacred. I saw God's presence everywhere. I wondered how I had missed seeing this for so long. Then I realised that the world hadn't changed; I had been changed.

True, there is evil in the world, but God's love is always working in the world too. He calls us to repent and to seek clean hearts. Living in unrepentant sin gives each day a dark and ominous feeling. However, with repentance and forgiveness, every day takes on a bright, clean appearance. The change can be like beginning a new life.

Prayer: *Dear God, fill our hearts with your love so that we can share it with people we encounter. Amen*

Thought for the day: God's love fills us with the light of new life.

Gale A. Richards (Iowa, US)

God the Mother

Read Hosea 11:1–4

As a mother comforts her child, so I will comfort you.
Isaiah 66:13 (NRSV)

'My translation says something different here,' my friend said. We were leading a discussion on Psalm 91 and its comparison of God to a fortress that can protect and shield us. But we began talking about the bird imagery in verse 4. Our German language Bibles had contained very different imagery. One translation, a paraphrase edition, compared God to a mother hen; the other, Luther's translation, spoke of God as a bird with strong, sheltering wings. My friend liked the image of God as an eagle with strong wings to shelter us. I agreed at the time; but the more I thought about it, the more I realised that I actually disagreed.

As I get older, I appreciate more and more everything my mother has done for me: the sleep lost; the hours spent playing with me; driving me everywhere and helping me with homework; the laundry washed; the wisdom offered; the prayers prayed. How much she must have given up so that she could always be there for me!

I love the image of God as a mother, there for her children all the time, caring for them and sacrificing for them. God is our protector; but he is also our comforter.

Prayer: *God, our protector and comforter, thank you for caring for us, your children. Thank you for images that give us a deeper understanding of you. Amen*

Thought for the day: God is both mother and father for us.

Alina Kanaski (Pennsylvania, US)

Unchanging Values

Read Micah 6:6–8

What does the Lord require of you? To act justly and to love mercy and to walk humbly with your God.
Micah 6:8 (NIV)

When asking for directions to a certain shop, a friend who was new to our town asked me, 'Is it on the right side of the street or the left side?' I replied that it depended on where he was coming from. 'If you're coming from the sugar factory, it's on the left side of the street.' That didn't seem to help, so I just said that it's on the west side of the street. West—like north, east and south—does not depend on where you're coming from. It is fixed and unchanging.

Some parts of our lives can be a matter of individual choice: clothes, food, hobbies. But for Christians, compassion, honesty, peace-seeking and justice are non-negotiable. We are called by Jesus to practise compassion and honesty, to seek peace and justice, and to be loyal to God in every situation. These ways of Christian living are as unchanging as the cardinal points on the compass. They are the standards by which Jesus lived and to which he has called us to live.

Prayer: *Thank you, Holy One, for all of the opportunities you put before us. Help us to honour Jesus' call for peace and compassion as we pray, 'Our Father in heaven, hallowed be your name, your kingdom come, your will be done, on earth as it is in heaven. Give us today our daily bread. And forgive us our debts, as we also have forgiven our debtors. And lead us not into temptation, but deliver us from the evil one.'* Amen*

Thought for the day: Jesus calls me to a life of compassion, honesty, peace and justice.

Philip A. Rice (Michigan, US)

        * Matthew 6:9–13 (NIV)

Unflinching Devotion

Read Psalm 149:1–5

Whatever your task, put yourselves into it, as done for the Lord and not for your masters, since you know that from the Lord you will receive the inheritance as your reward; you serve the Lord Christ.
Colossians 3:23–24 (NRSV)

My elder brother takes great delight in his service to God. Most week-ends, he wakes up early and joins the women in our local church in keeping the chapel clean. He is also zealous in his participation in the church's drama group, always ministering to the glory of God.

As he has served, God has opened a new door for him. He was awarded a scholarship to study for a master's degree in agriculture at the University of Kent. After completing his 14-month-long studies, he returned to Nigeria and continued with his unflinching devotion to ministry for God.

One Sunday morning, the women in our church, who were inspired by his committed service to the church and to God, decided to honour him, conferring on him a 'disciple of the year' award. My family was amazed at this great honour.

Through my brother's example, the words of the scripture quoted above came alive for all of us in a new way. His continued dedication has inspired a younger generation to devote their time in service to God and to their brothers and sisters wherever they find them.

Prayer: *Gracious God, help us to work humbly in your service so that all may know that you are God. Amen*

Thought for the day: God rewards the faithful with joy.

Ibifubara Okoseimiema (Rivers State, Nigeria)

No One to Help

Read John 5:1–9

At once the man was cured; he picked up his mat and walked.
John 5:9 (NIV)

It was the Sabbath. Jesus and the disciples were in Jerusalem when they encountered a number of people who were blind, sick and lame waiting by the pool of Bethesda. These people believed that its water possessed healing powers. While walking by the pool, Jesus encountered a man who had been ill for a long time. Jesus showed mercy to the man and healed him.

Jesus' encounter with the man by the pool tugs at my heart. When Jesus asked him if he wanted to get well, the man replied 'I have no one to help me into the pool when the water is stirred. While I am trying to get in, someone else goes down ahead of me.' When I read these words, I picture the man trying to get into the pool and missing his opportunity every time—for 38 years—until the day Jesus walked by and the man's life changed for ever.

This passage from John's Gospel reminds us that no matter how hard we try, some things cannot be accomplished without the help of Christ. Too often I have tried to succeed on my own, only to have someone '[go] down ahead of me'. Eventually, Jesus has come along to tell me to 'pick up [my] mat' and to trust his way and his power for my life.

Prayer: *Father God, thank you for being with us; we cannot make it on our own. Amen*

Thought for the day: Christ stands ready to help me.

Sherri Tuck (Virginia, US)

Seeds of Faith

Read Matthew 19:13–15

Train children in the way they should go; when they grow old, they won't depart from it.
Proverbs 22:6 (CEB)

My parents were of Armenian heritage. My mother's name was Zabel, or Isabel. I give thanks to God for my parents and their legacy of family prayer.

I remember with fondness each night when my mother would place a worn carpet on the floor. She, my father, my three siblings and I would sit in a circle as my mother read a daily devotional. Then she would open her Bible and read the scripture in her language. We all listened attentively. We would offer our reflections, and then my mother would ask us to join in a prayer.

Today I begin each day by reading a portion of scripture along with the daily devotional from *El Aposento Alto*, the Spanish language edition of *The Upper Room*. The meditations and life experiences of our brothers and sisters around the world enrich my life. I treasure the seeds of faith my mother planted in us—the discipline of devotional reflection, Bible reading and prayer. Her great faith continues to inspire me and keeps me focused on God's will for my life.

Prayer: *Creator God, thank you for the teachings and guidance of those whose faith has created the foundation of our own spiritual life. Amen*

Thought for the day: How might I plant the seed of faith in another?

Rebeca Boyadjian Fahmazian (Uruguay)

The New Me

Read 2 Corinthians 5:17–21

If anyone is in Christ, there is a new creation: everything old has passed away; see, everything has become new!
2 Corinthians 5:17 (NRSV)

One of my favourite places to study the Bible and to spend my devotional time is in the room adjoining our kitchen, near a fireplace and lots of windows. In this peaceful and picturesque space, I can see deer grazing, pine trees swaying in the breeze and birds feeding. As I look into the morning sky, my attention is drawn to the moving clouds that are constantly changing in size and shape.

The cloud formations remind me that God is always creating and recreating, making all things new. Since Christ came into my life, I have radically changed. The old me is being transformed into a new creation. Daily I am dying to my old self—the me that tried to live life in my own strength and power. This has not been easy. My life is a work in progress. I am not yet what I ought to be, but thanks to God I am not what I used to be. Through God's amazing grace and transforming power, he is shaping me into the image of Jesus Christ.

Prayer: *Creator God, thank you for looking beyond our faults and seeing our need for salvation. Forgive and guide us daily as we seek to grow in the likeness of Christ. Amen*

Thought for the day: Abundant life begins with accepting God's love and saving grace.

John I. Penn (Georgia, US)

Choosing Joy

Read Psalm 118:26–29

Rejoice always, pray continually, give thanks in all circumstances; for this is God's will for you in Christ Jesus.
1 Thessalonians 5:16–18 (NIV)

I spent one summer in the Upper Peninsula of Michigan planning and leading children's activities. Before I arrived I imagined that the other staff members would be friendly, that the children would behave angelically and that I would spend my free time at the lake.

As it turned out, the staff rarely acknowledged me, the children refused to listen to directions and ran wild, and the weather was cold, overcast and rainy most of the month. I became bitter and discontented as I longed for the summer that I had imagined and felt I deserved.

I went for a walk on one of the rare sunny days, bundled up in a thick fleece, and stood on the bridge over the cove. As I looked at God's creation I was astounded by the contrast between the tiny detail in the flower petals and the massive 100-year-old trees. I exchanged my discontent for gratitude and joy.

Every moment of the day, we have a choice: to compare life to our expectations or to thank God for what we have been given. We can rejoice in the small adventures and surprises that God hides inside every day for us to discover if we only give that day a chance.

Prayer: *Dear God, fill our hearts with your peace and joy, and teach us to treat each day as a gift. Amen*

Thought for the day: I can choose to give thanks joyfully for God's love each day.

Mackenzie Jagger (Michigan, US)

The Ice Cream Man

Read 1 Corinthians 13:1–13
If I have a faith that can move mountains, but do not have love, I am nothing.
1 Corinthians 13:2 (NIV)

When I was around six or seven the ice cream man would come in his white van with the chimes ringing out—a signal for the children to bring their money to buy ice cream. I would hang back because there was no spare money to be had at my house. One day the ice cream man called me over and asked if that was my vegetable patch in our garden. I said yes, and then he told me that he loved carrots—and that if I would bring him some from our garden, he would give me ice cream. So I ran to the garden, pulled some carrots and went back to collect my ice cream. We continued the carrots-for-ice cream exchange for a good while.

It was only later in my life that I realised what grace the ice cream man had shown me. He didn't make me feel as if I was taking a hand-out or that I was to be pitied. He treated me with dignity in front of my friends. Without my knowing it, he was showing me a love like God's.

Simple acts of mercy can help someone get through a tough day or even a tough childhood. I have never forgotten the ice cream man's gift to me. When we act with love toward others, we echo Paul's words, 'the greatest of these is love'.

Prayer: *Dear Lord, we thank you for the people who have shown us your love. Help us to be the hands and feet of Christ to those who need us. Amen*

Thought for the day: Compassionate acts demonstrate God's love.

Grace Epperson (Michigan, US)

A Mother's Gift

Read Ecclesiastes 3:1–8

There is a time for everything, and a season for every activity under the heavens: a time to be born and a time to die.

Ecclesiastes 3:1–2 (NIV)

My mother died on Mother's Day—the day she and I usually celebrated by remembering when she gave birth to me and heard my first breath. But on that Mother's Day I was telling my mother how much I loved her as she drew her last breath. I kept thinking about all the priceless lessons she taught me, such as the importance of studying the Bible.

In another time of loss, when my husband died, grief overwhelmed me. I fell into major depression. I had to give up my career, and I contemplated suicide as I could see no end to my deepening unhappiness. Slowly, however, with the right medication and help from a good therapist, I began to work toward better health—spiritual, physical and emotional. As I recovered, another of my mother's lessons helped me: the road of life may be difficult and seem impassable, but God will be with me all throughout my life's journey—even when I do not feel him near me.

Each Mother's Day I now celebrate the memory of my mother and thank God for her legacy of unwavering faith and for the lessons she taught me by the example of her daily life and walk with God.

Prayer: *Dear God, thank you for the lessons we have learned from those whose faith is unwavering. Amen*

Thought for the day: I can find God's presence in my life every day.

Alice M. Nathan (Missouri, US)

Keep Your Heart in Tune

Read John 15:1–17

Jesus said, 'Abide in me as I abide in you. Just as the branch cannot bear fruit by itself unless it abides in the vine, neither can you unless you abide in me.'

John 15:4 (NRSV)

I woke up one morning, singing a song that my classmates and I had sung together many years before. The song emphasised the importance of praying in the morning, afternoon and evening to 'keep your heart in tune'.* I wondered what it means to 'keep your heart in tune'. As I searched for answers, I thought about tuning in each day to the TV or radio. I have learned that they are best when tuned to the right frequency.

As human beings created by God we are at our best when our hearts are tuned in to Jesus Christ. In John 15:1–8, Jesus uses the image of the vine and the branches to urge his disciples to stay connected to him. He is the source of new life.

The verse quoted above reminds us that the life of the branch is guaranteed only when it is connected to the vine. Branches not only receive life from the vine, they share its identity. In the same way, believers connected to Christ, the vine, begin to mirror him as he gives them new life. Connection to Jesus enables us to be the people God intends us to be.

Prayer: *Dear God, help us to tune our hearts to Jesus Christ, the source of life. Amen*

Thought for the day: I am at my best when I am connected to Jesus Christ.

Maaraidzo E. Mutambara (Mutare, Zimbabwe)

        * 'Whisper a prayer', words and music anonymous

Excuses, Excuses

Read Exodus 3:7–12

[God] said, 'I will be with you; and this shall be the sign for you that it is I who sent you: when you have brought the people out of Egypt, you shall worship God on this mountain.'
Exodus 3:12 (NRSV)

I have many flaws, doubts and fears and, all too often, I discover something new that I cannot do very well. My typical response is to spend my free time lying in bed watching TV. I cannot fail there unless I go to sleep and fall out of the bed. Sometimes I use my weaknesses as an excuse not to do something. Then I can say, 'I can't do that because I'm too—.'

Many people in the Bible made excuses, including Moses. In today's reading, God sees the oppression of the Israelites and wants Moses to lead them out of Egypt. Moses protests, 'Who am I that I should go to Pharaoh, and bring the Israelites out of Egypt?' Moses' excuse sounds a lot like the excuses I make. 'I can't do it. I'm not good enough. You're going to have to ask someone else.' But God reassures Moses, and me, 'I will be with you.'

Sometimes we focus on our inadequacies and think that we are not clever enough, talented enough or eloquent enough. But God doesn't make us cleverer or more talented or more articulate. Instead, he promises to remain with us, which is all we need.

Prayer: *Dear God, please continue to be with us and give us all we need to do your will. Amen*

Thought for the day: God does not erase my flaws but goes with me and fills me with courage.

Bob La Forge (New Jersey, US)

Small Deeds

Read John 6:1–13

Here is a boy with five small barley loaves and two small fish, but how far will they go among so many?
John 6:9 (NIV)

Early one morning while watering the plants on my porch I noticed that my favourite hanging plant was wilting. The blossoms were beginning to fade. I had only a little water left in my watering can, but I poured that on the plant, intending to come back later with more. In my busy day, I forgot to return to the plant.

Much later, when I went back out to the porch, I noticed that my once wilted plant had revived—the beautiful blooms were full and glorious again! It only took a few drops of water to bring back its beauty.

I realised that living our faith can work in a similar way. We may feel that if we can't do something big or if we don't have a lot to contribute, we cannot help someone. But many times, small gestures can make a big difference in someone's faith journey. One kind word spoken at the right time can turn everything around. Just like the boy's offering of his barley loaves and small fish in today's reading, a small deed done in the name of God can produce a miracle.

Prayer: *Dear God, help us to share our gifts—no matter how small they may seem. Thank you for giving us the gifts that can help produce miracles in others' lives. Amen*

Thought for the day: I can share God's love with a small act of kindness.

Mary Beth Rademaker (North Carolina, US)

A Time to Wait

Read Isaiah 40:28–31
The Lord waits to be gracious to you.
Isaiah 30:18 (NRSV)

As I worried recently about the results of medical tests, I thought of all the occasions in my life that have required waiting. I have waited for a spouse to return from war, waited for my child to be born, waited for loved ones to regain health after illness or surgery and waited with grieving people. I often felt impatient and anxious knowing that I was not in control of the situation or its outcome. Even waiting for a happy occasion such as a wedding or a holiday can include anxious moments.

By reading scripture like the verse quoted above, I have learned that God understands our frustration with waiting. Today's reading encourages us to be patient and wait for God. I now realise that God is always present, even when we are waiting and uncertain about the results of our wait. We can pray as we are 'still before the Lord and [waiting] patiently for him' (Psalm 37:7). This kind of waiting can replace our anxiety with peace.

Prayer: *Heavenly Father, thank you for your guidance and strength in times of uncertainty. Teach us to be patient and peaceful as we rest in your word. Amen*

Thought for the day: God waits with me.

Lois M. Baker (Arkansas, US)

No Regrets

Read Philippians 3:7-16

Do not say, 'Why were the old days better than these?' For it is not wise to ask such questions.
Ecclesiastes 7:10 (NIV)

While doing some spring cleaning, I came across a dust-covered bag. I expected it to be filled with useless old papers. Instead I was surprised to find old letters, cards and photographs from around the time I left high school.

Life has not always been kind to me, yet in many ways God has blessed me. Still, as I looked at these mementos from when my life was full of promise and potential, I felt a pang of regret for what I perceived as a life of failure and mediocrity. I yearned for that earlier time when things seemed simpler and safer. If only I could change the poor decisions I have made, I thought, I might be able to reverse their bitter effects.

In truth, life was not easier then. Through these hard years I have matured, and God has taught me wisdom, building me into a person of faith. From our new birth of salvation, we journey onward toward our heavenly home. The goal doesn't lie behind us; there is no benefit in going back. Our life in Christ may be many things, but it will never be a life of regret.

Prayer: *Wise and loving God, thank you for freeing us from the past. Lead us on toward your purpose for our lives. Amen*

Thought for the day: My future in Christ outshines the regrets of my past.

Jeff Riley (Oklahoma, US)

My Daughter's Example

Read Matthew 18:1–5

I say to you, Love your enemies and pray for those who persecute you, so that you may be children of your Father in heaven.
Matthew 5:44–45 (NRSV)

One day, my young daughter came home from school and told me, 'My best friend is going to have a birthday party, and she has already given out the invitations.' I asked her whether she was invited. She answered, 'No. She said she forgot to invite me. But it is OK.' Without sadness or apparent disappointment, she chatted happily about school.

I remembered my own disappointment and anger when one of my colleagues did not invite me to her birthday party. I resented her for this.

But Jesus reminds us that we should change and become like little children. My daughter's response was a strong example of the attitude Jesus wants us to have. She did not take offence and did not dwell on her friend's mistake. Often we are unable to do these simple things, so we fill the world with revenge, murder and war. Inspired by my daughter's example, I knelt down and prayed for God's forgiveness and guidance.

Prayer: *Dear Lord Jesus, help us to follow your teachings. As you forgive us, help us forgive those who have hurt us. Amen*

Thought for the day: Jesus, our example, forgave those who hurt him.

Amy Sutikdja (North Rhine-Westphalia, Germany)

What Does a Neighbour Do?

Read Luke 10:29–37
'The King will reply, "Truly I tell you, whatever you did for one of the least of these brothers and sisters of mine, you did for me."'
Matthew 25:40 (NIV)

When I visit the city near my home, I am alarmed at the large number of men, women, and sometimes even children sleeping on pavements and in shop doorways. Then I remember that in Jesus' parable of the good Samaritan, the true neighbour attends to the needs of others.

Do I stop and attend to the needs of these individuals? Occasionally I do, but I admit that I often pass by—grateful for various initiatives that are designed to meet their needs. However, as I step around these suffering people, God reminds me of Jesus' command for us to care for the least among us—whether we do that as individuals, as a society or as the church.

Many of our brothers and sisters live in desperate poverty. When I recall Jesus' story of the good Samaritan, I am moved to renew my commitment to work with Christian compassion for the well-being of all my neighbours.

Prayer: *Dear Father, help us always remember your command to love our neighbours as ourselves. Continue to fill us with compassion for the least among us. As Jesus taught us, we pray, 'Father, hallowed be your name, your kingdom come. Give us each our daily bread. Forgive us our sins, for we also forgive everyone who sins against us. And lead us not into temptation.'* Amen*

Thought for the day: How can I be a 'good Samaritan' to my neighbours today?

Scott Martin (New Jersey, US)

PRAYER FOCUS: PEOPLE WHO ARE HOMELESS
* Luke 11:2–4 (NIV)

What's Next?

Read Exodus 3:1–12
We are God's handiwork, created in Christ Jesus to do good works, which God prepared in advance for us to do.
Ephesians 2:10 (NIV)

Moses was rescued as a baby and grew up in the palace of the great Pharaoh, receiving all the privileges of royalty. But then, in a terrible, misguided attempt at justice, he murdered a man and ultimately fled for his own life. By the time of today's reading he was tending sheep out in the middle of nowhere. Then God gave Moses a new purpose.

Some of us may worry that our important or most fulfilling days are behind us. We may have left a good career to bring up our children or may be looking around at an 'empty nest'. Perhaps our skills are no longer valued in an industry because of technological advances, or we are facing the unknowns of retirement. No matter where we are in life, God has significant work for each of us to do. It may be something as simple as sending notes of encouragement or as complex as working for our government to bring about economic change or the resolution of conflict. Whatever the case, as he did with Moses, God says to us, 'I will be with you' (Exodus 3:12).

Prayer: *Dear God, help us to serve you faithfully in every stage of our lives. In Jesus' name we pray. Amen*

Thought for the day: Am I willing to say yes to God's purpose for me?

Gail Parker (Maryland, US)

The Puzzle Pieces of Life

Read Ecclesiastes 3:9–14

What do workers gain from their toil? I have seen the burden God has laid on the human race… yet no one can fathom what God has done from beginning to end.
Ecclesiastes 3:9–11 (NIV)

When I take my son to the toyshop to buy a new jigsaw puzzle, he makes his choice based on the picture on the outside of the box—the potential beauty that it can become. But when we first open the box, the puzzle looks nothing like the picture on the outside; it is simply jumbled-up pieces in a bag.

We all face trials and tribulations that can leave us puzzled by worry, anger or sadness. We may feel broken like the puzzle pieces in the bag. But God can always see the bigger picture—the picture on the outside of the box. As today's reading says, '[God] has made everything beautiful in its time' (Ecclesiastes 3:11).

Although the burdens of life will arise, God takes the broken pieces of our pain, sadness, worry and grief and works in them to create something beautiful and whole. He knows the potential we hold. When our hearts are heavy and our strength is low, we can trust that with God, our puzzles will be completed.

Prayer: *Dear Lord, help us to trust that you are always at work in our lives. Amen*

Thought for the day: My life's puzzle is beautiful in the eyes of God.

Chelsia Calvert (Texas, US)

God is with us

Read Matthew 26:36–39

Jesus prayed, 'My Father, if it is possible, may this cup be taken from me. Yet not as I will, but as you will.'
Matthew 26:39 (KJV)

I keep a written copy of the verse quoted above in my wallet because reading it helps me to keep life in perspective. Too many times I have allowed arrogance and pride to dictate how I have approached difficult situations. Treating God's word like a lucky charm I kept in my pocket, I would say to myself, I've got this—thinking I had control of everything. If life got really tough, only then would I call on God and ask for the strength to make it through.

Once I began reading the Bible regularly, I came to understand that if I rely on God's strength at all times—not just when I am desperate—God's grace and power will guide me through all the different circumstances of my life.

These words from Matthew's Gospel taught me that even Jesus had a moment when he felt overwhelmed and needed to call on his Father for strength. If the Son of God needed to call on his Father in his moment of need, then certainly we too can call upon God to lead us every step of the way.

Prayer: *Dear God, thank you for guiding us through life, especially through challenges and overwhelming circumstances. Amen*

Thought for the day: I will trust the path that God lays before me.

Christopher C. Rowe (North Carolina, US)

A Second Chance

Read John 7:53—8:11

Jesus said, 'Neither do I condemn you. Go your way, and from now on do not sin again.'
John 8:11 (NRSV)

I often think back to mistakes I made both in the distant past and just yesterday. Why did I make that stupid remark? Why did I gossip about another person? And then I start thinking about larger life choices: wrong turns I have taken or times when I have done self-destructive things.

Then I think of how Jesus treated the woman caught in adultery in today's reading. First he protected her from certain death at the hands of authorities by asking them to consider their own sins. And then, amazingly, he didn't condemn her. Jesus gave her a second chance and the opportunity to learn from her mistakes.

When I do something I know is harmful to myself or others, I can remember that Jesus refrains from judging me, but calls me to make better decisions and sin no more. He gives me a second chance—and sometimes many more than that—every time.

Prayer: *Dear Lord, thank you for giving us second chances to follow your ways. Help us to learn from our mistakes as we seek to follow you more faithfully. Amen*

Thought for the day: Jesus always offers me a second chance.

Abigail Gary (New Jersey, US)

God Cares For Us

Read James 2:14–17
Faith by itself, if it has no works, is dead.
James 2:17 (NRSV)

During Perestroika, a time of political and economic instability in the Soviet Union, many Russian people, fearing for their lives, left their birthplaces, their property and their homes and fled to other places where they could live in safety. Our family moved from Chechnya to the Krasnodar region. We lived in a tent in extreme poverty and need. Our situation was hopeless. God seemed to have abandoned us.

One day, the Methodist minister visited us. He saw how hard our life was, and we talked with him for a long time. I told him about our lack of money and food. I told him we were cold. At the end of our conversation, I asked him to pray with me for my family and our future; but he refused. 'I haven't got time to pray now,' he said and left quickly.

The minister hurriedly went to a shop, bought some essential provisions, sorted out some warm winter children's clothes and brought them all to us. When the children had been fed and were feeling warm again, he said, 'Now I am ready to pray with you and to thank God for his generosity. You see, God cares about you and provides for your needs.'

Prayer: *Dear Lord, thank you for remembering poor, needy and hungry people. Help us to show them care and generosity. Amen*

Thought for the day: Sometimes God answers prayers through our actions.

Tatyana Azyavina (Krasnodar, Russia)

Complain or Contribute?

Read Philippians 2:12–18

Let us… make every effort to do what leads to peace and to mutual edification.
Romans 14:19 (NIV)

One Sunday morning after worship I overheard a brief conversation between two parishioners. One of the men said, 'I didn't get much out of the service. Did you?' 'Not much,' the other replied. It was disconcerting to hear, though I have to admit that I have made similar complaints.

Often we go to church wondering what we are going to get out of it. But we don't ask ourselves what we can put into it.

Perhaps our experience of church can be re-energised if we complain less and spend that energy encouraging one another. One Sunday a woman whose husband was in hospital approached me as I was entering the church. She told me excitedly that her husband had spoken to one of his nurses about his faith in Jesus Christ. After he had prayed with her, she accepted Jesus as her Saviour. She then shared her experience with others. Her excitement was contagious. My own spirit was lifted and I responded, 'Praise the Lord!'

Her story showed me that we can contribute to the community of faith in many ways. We can compliment others for their service, volunteer when opportunities arise, give generously, seek out and help to meet the needs of others, and give assurance of our prayers.

Prayer: *Dear God, forgive us for our self-centred attitudes. Show us how we can encourage others. Amen*

Thought for the day: How could less complaining and more caring change my community of faith?

Wayne Greenawalt (Illinois, US)

Loss or Gain?

Read Isaiah 55:8–11

*'My thoughts are not your thoughts, neither are your ways my ways,'
declares the Lord.*
Isaiah 55:8 (NIV)

'Kim, you're a good employee and the residents love you, but due
to budget cuts, you are going to be made redundant.' I was shocked
to hear these words from the manager of the care home where I was
working at the time. I was sad because I would miss the friends I had
grown to love there. However, I had been praying for a new adventure,
and God used the loss of my job to launch me into full-time ministry
with people in Romania who were elderly and homeless.

God's ways are higher than mine, so although I didn't realise it, my
job at the care home had prepared me for my new work with at-risk
elderly people in another country. God used the job I had just lost,
which I had never expected to take in the first place, to prepare me for
the next season of my life.

When something happens that we don't understand, we can choose
to trust God, who sees the big picture of our lives. In each experience of
our lives and every challenging situation we face, we can trust that God
is working for good.

Prayer: *Dear God, help us to trust you with whatever happens each
day of our lives. Amen*

Thought for the day: God is always working for my good.

Kim Jackson (North Carolina, US)

Why God, Why?

Read Mark 14:32–42
Carry each other's burdens.
Galatians 6:2 (CEB)

I have never understood why people suffer or prayers seem to go unanswered, and I probably never will. I do, however, find comfort in knowing that I'm not alone in my lack of understanding or in my suffering.

In today's reading, Jesus himself broke down in the midst of his suffering and begged God to intervene. He then questioned God's silence when he needed him the most (see Mark 15:34).

Jesus was no stranger to fear, loneliness, desperation, pain, anguish and confusion. He felt them all on the cross. They are emotions shared by all humans. God doesn't think less of us for having those feelings or expressing them out loud. They don't make us less faithful; they make us human.

It may take courage to admit any of these feelings, but doing so binds us together and makes us stronger. There will be a time, however, when we will leave all this behind us and dwell with God where none of this world's sorrows exist (see Revelation 21:3–4). In the meantime, we can extend to others the same compassion and love we so desperately need by standing together in prayer and offering encouragement.

Prayer: *Dear God, open our eyes today to see those around us who are suffering so we can ease their burdens. Amen*

Thought for the day: Because of my faith, I am not alone.

Esther L. Bonner (California, US)

'The Price Is Paid'

Read Isaiah 53:1–9
You are not your own; you were bought at a price.
1 Corinthians 6:19–20 (NIV)

The wind was brisk as we stood huddled and cold on the town steps one evening in April. We were thankful we had remembered to wear our heavy coats, gloves and scarves; and though we were not professional singers, every word we sang was from the heart: 'All in the April evening, April airs were abroad… I saw the sheep with their lambs and thought on the Lamb of God.'*

The shoppers hurried by. No doubt they wished to be home as quickly as possible in front of a warm fire. With their heads down, they hardly noticed us.

The bread shop opposite us was still open, so some shoppers popped in to buy the cakes and breads that were tastefully displayed. But as the shoppers reached for a purse or wallet, they were told, 'The price is paid.' They owed nothing for their purchases.

As a Christian outreach group we had arranged to pay for the purchases that evening in an effort to bring home the message of Easter: it wasn't just the bread and the cakes that were free. Because Jesus paid the price for our sins, we are forgiven and free to live a new life following the way of Christ!

Prayer: *O Lord, we thank you for your loving sacrifice that frees us to live as forgiven people. Amen*

Thought for the day: How will I thank God for the gift of salvation?

Carol Purves (Carlisle, England)

PRAYER FOCUS: CHURCH CHOIR MEMBERS   41
* 'All in the April evening (Katharine Tynan and Hugh S. Robertson)

Pentecost

Read Acts 2:1–12

When the day of Pentecost was fully come, they were all with one accord in one place.

Acts 2:1 (KJV)

I have been teaching my Sunday school pupils about Pentecost. I tell them how I relate to the first disciples who were amazed by the way the Holy Spirit allows everyone to follow Christ regardless of native language.

Every few years we visit my in-laws who have a house in the Black Forest region of Germany. Even though I do not speak German, I enjoy attending church services there. The sermon, music and prayers are all in a language I don't speak, but I feel at home and understand without needing translation. It is as if the Holy Spirit allows me to feel peace, love and sincerity in the way people speak, in the music sung by joyful choir, and in the prayers. Even though I do not understand the words, I can tell what is going on in the service by the way it is said. For instance, I know when the Lord's Prayer is being said or that we will be singing a familiar hymn when the organ starts to play the melody.

I encourage anyone travelling abroad to find a local church and go to a service. Through familiar practices and the power of the Holy Spirit, we can understand without knowing the language.

Prayer: *Creator God, thank you for the Holy Spirit who allows all people everywhere to understand your word and worship in their own languages. Help us to welcome all visitors and invite them to worship with us. Amen*

Thought for the day: God can hear my prayers no matter what language I speak.

David John Walker (Ohio, US)

Flower Pies

Read John 3:16–21

For God so loved the world that he gave his one and only Son, that whoever believes in him shall not perish but have eternal life.
John 3:16 (NIV)

When I was young, I could have won a medal for making fantastic 'flower pies'. I would spend countless hours gathering wide varieties of stones from my grandma's driveway and placing them neatly in the old pie tins that she supplied. I especially loved smoothing the top of the 'pie' and decorating it with the most beautiful flowers I could find. I vividly remember picking the prettiest, most colourful blossoms in Grandma's yard. She never once complained that I was wasting her most beautiful flowers on my creative projects. She willingly sacrificed her best to make me happy.

The love my grandma shared with me reminds me of God's selfless love. He gave up the very best for me also—his Son, Jesus Christ. The Bible reminds me that God relinquished the greatest thing possible so that we might be saved. He demonstrated how to be self-denying and gave us a pattern of selfless love. When we put another's needs, comfort or happiness before our own, we are reflecting the true love God shows each of us.

Prayer: *Dear Lord, help us to show selfless love to others as you have done for us. In Jesus' name we pray. Amen*

Thought for the day: God gave the very best for me. How can I give my best for others?

Alisha Ritchie (North Carolina, US)

Stronger on My Knees

Read Romans 5:1–5

Daniel knelt down, prayed, and praised his God three times [each] day.
Daniel 6:10 (CEB)

Having put all five of us children and all our belongings in the cart, my father helped my mother to get onto the water buffalo and led us to his church service about five kilometres across the river. It was raining hard, and the trail was muddy, knee-deep in some places. Father prodded the water buffalo to go faster because we had to cross the river before it became impassable. Going up the riverbank on the steep and slippery trail was difficult. Suddenly my younger brother cried out, 'Father, look! The buffalo is kneeling. It can't pull us up anymore!' Father looked back at us in the cart. 'Don't worry, son,' he said. 'The buffalo is strongest when it kneels.'

I watched the buffalo as it struggled on the slippery trail one step at a time. It would stop, kneel, strain, get up slowly and pull, until we were over the top. The animal's strength came from kneeling, just as Father had said. Each time it knelt, it pulled us up farther and faster.

That was many years ago. I often think of the buffalo as I pass through difficult times in my personal life. I, too, have discovered extraordinary strength when I get down on my knees in prayer.

Prayer: *Dear God, help us find strength in prayer. Amen*

Thought for the day: We are strongest when we are on our knees in prayer.

Phebe Gamata Crismo (Bulacan, Philippines)

Hold Nothing Back

Read Mark 14:3–9

A woman came with an alabaster jar of very costly ointment of nard, and she broke open the jar and poured the ointment on [Jesus'] head.
Mark 14:3 (NSRV)

My son gave me a big bottle of my favourite aftershave. I treasure this gift, and as the months go by, I use just a little of it because I want it to last longer. But the woman in our reading for today wasn't concerned about conserving her costly perfume. She broke open the jar so that nothing could stop its flow to Jesus.

We often say that we will give our all for God, but usually we give ourselves in a controlled way. We pour out a little here and a little there, thinking that many will see our good works and give glory to God (Matthew 5:16). God wants all our attention, our focus, our gifts, our talents and our thoughts—all of us.

I remember the woman in today's reading not because of the cost of her gift or because of her humility, both of which are worthy of attention. I remember her because she shattered the jar and poured all its contents on Jesus. She held nothing back.

When we give ourselves to God, we are offering a priceless gift. Will we give God only a little here and a little there, or will we break ourselves open and pour ourselves out to him?

Prayer: *Dear Lord, thank you for the precious gift of your Son, Jesus Christ. Help us to be open in giving ourselves to you. Amen*

Thought for the day: Today I will look for ways to pour myself out for God.

David J. Schreffler (Pennsylvania, US)

PRAYER FOCUS: SOMEONE CALLED TO A NEW MINISTRY

God is Good

Read 2 Corinthians 12:6–10

Give thanks to the Lord, for he is good. His love endures for ever.
Psalm 136:1 (NIV)

Several years ago, I was diagnosed with rheumatoid arthritis. A few years after my diagnosis, I went through months of debilitating pain. At that time, I was unable to do much at all. Every joint hurt—even my cheekbones and my jaw. But through it all, I knew God was with me and would take care of me.

Previously I had battled depression and the death of my fiancé, and I had experienced God's goodness through the support of others and the encouragement from scripture such as the verse quoted above. This new pain was difficult, but God's care made it more tolerable and gave me joy. Some of my friends were baffled. They couldn't understand how I could have such joy in the midst of my suffering. After all, wasn't God the one who was allowing this? I explained to them that because of God's tender care in my darkest hours, I have come to know that he is good and remains a steadfast, caring presence at all times.

God is good, even when we lose our jobs. God is good, even when a marriage fails. God is good, even when a loved one dies. And yes, God is good, even when we have debilitating pain. God is good all the time, and it is precisely our faith in his unceasing goodness that can give us outrageous and contagious joy. God is truly good all the time!

Prayer: *Thank you, Lord, for being so good. Help us to have faith in your goodness so that we can share our joy with others even when life is difficult. Amen*

Thought for the day: Even when circumstances are bad, God is good.

Tina Chaves (New Jersey, US)

Growing Potential

Read Matthew 13:24–30

The steadfast love of the Lord never ceases, his mercies never come to an end; they are new every morning.
Lamentations 3:22–23 (NRSV)

For several years, wild violets have grown in part of my herb garden. Then it finally occurred to me that violets are weeds. They may be beautiful, but I was allowing them to sap the vital nutrients from the soil to the detriment of my herbs. I had compromised the integrity of my garden for the sake of the violets.

Sin, like weeds, can come into our lives beautifully packaged and seemingly harmless. And it robs us of the spiritual nutrients we need to grow. I wondered where I had compromised my spiritual life by letting sin grow. What pretty package did it come in? For starters, I like to think I am self-sufficient. I don't always ask God for guidance, and sometimes I forget to read my Bible.

Thankfully, God provides new mercies every morning and I am forgiven. Just as I pulled out the violets that prevented my herbs from growing to their full potential, with God's guidance, we are able to make choices and to change behaviour so that we will no longer compromise our spiritual growth.

Prayer: *Gracious God, forgive our failings. Help us to uproot sin from our hearts and minds and use our hands, feet and voices to spread your good news. Amen*

Thought for the day: How do the compromises and choices I make impact my spiritual growth?

Lynne Jamison (Pennsylvania, US)

God's Transforming Love

Read Romans 12:1–2

Do not conform yourselves to the standards of this world, but let God transform you inwardly by a complete change of your mind.
Romans 12:2 (GNB)

We had returned to Aberdovey in mid-Wales for our summer holiday. Very little appeared to have changed in the seaside village: the bleached beaches, muted dunes and the estuary all looked the same, though their colours were changed by wind and tide.

At the parish church of St Peter, a year ago I had responded to a request for volunteers to help with the repair of an altar frontal, a beautiful but worn purple cloth. Its restoration looked as if it would be a long and hard task under the guidance of an expert, so this year I was amazed to hear that there was soon to be an exhibition of the frontal, which had been completed, along with other works in progress. Proudly the church volunteers showed me the completed frontal's new embroidery and jewels; it appeared as good as new.

This experience reminded me that often there appears to be little change in our lives and that outwardly we look pretty much the same. Yet somehow God works slowly and patiently in our lives to change us from within, so difficulties are overcome and past mistakes redeemed. In our earthly lives we are his works in progress. If we allow it, we can be forgiven, renewed and ultimately transformed into something beautiful and precious to God.

Prayer: *Help us, Lord, by the power of your Spirit, to listen and respond, so that we may be transformed into what is pleasing in your sight. Amen*

Thought for the day: God is working to transform my life.

Faith Ford (Herefordshire, England)

United by One Love

Read Colossians 3:9–17

Above all, clothe yourselves with love, which binds everything together in perfect harmony.
Colossians 3:14 (NRSV)

Some friends and I went to a piano symphony concert in Pärnu, Estonia. The musicians played beautifully and it seemed to me as if time stood still. When I looked at the programme I noticed that all the young musicians were from different countries (Germany, China, North Korea, France and Austria). Despite the fact that everyone was from a different place, we all spoke the same language that night—the language of music.

In much the same way, when I read the meditations in *Mesto Vstrechi* (the Russian edition of *The Upper Room*) I feel a sense of unity with the authors of each meditation. We are all brothers and sisters in faith from different countries of the world, each speaking our own language and united by one love of our Lord. No borders or language barriers can divide us because God's love unites us all into one big church here on earth.

Prayer: *Dear Father, we are grateful for your love for each of your children. Teach us to love one another, however far apart we are, and always to pray for your many-peopled church on earth. As Jesus taught us, we pray, 'Our Father which art in heaven, Hallowed be thy name. Thy kingdom come. Thy will be done, as in heaven, so in earth. Give us day by day our daily bread. And forgive us our sins, for we also forgive every one that is indebted to us. And lead us not into temptation, but deliver us from evil.'* Amen*

Thought for the day: Our love unites us as brothers and sisters in Christ.

Nataliya Konstantinova (Pskov, Russia)

The Lord's Good Work

Read Matthew 25:31–46

Jesus said, 'Give to those who ask, and don't refuse those who wish to borrow from you.'
Matthew 5:42 (CEB)

One day as I was leaving the supermarket, a man recognised me from my teaching days. He introduced himself and asked if I could give him a lift to a nearby petrol station. On the way he told me about his broken truck and that he needed to borrow a little money to tow it to his friend's garage, where it would be fixed for free. Upon arrival, he asked to borrow just a bit more money for petrol. I wondered why he needed petrol for a broken truck.

This man had asked for a lift, money and finally more money. I said a silent prayer and gave him more than he asked for. He thanked me profusely and promised to pay me back with interest. As I drove off, I felt I had been conned.

Not until I prayed out loud, 'Lord, help that money to do good,' did I feel better about the situation. It didn't matter whether he was telling the truth about the truck. One of God's children was trying desperately to make it in the world—and he had asked me for help.

I have come to understand that helping someone and then expecting something in return is doing business, not showing God's love. I pray that my act of compassion did what it was meant to do: the Lord's good work.

Prayer: *Dear Lord, help us overcome our harsh judgement of others, and show us how to help when you call us to give assistance. In Jesus' name. Amen*

Thought for the day: Showing God's love through acts of compassion is its own reward.

Will Pepper (Mississippi, US)

God is Near

Read Psalm 63:1–11

God… earnestly I seek you; I thirst for you, my whole being longs for you, in a dry and parched land… On my bed I remember you; I think of you through the watches of the night. Because you are my help… I cling to you.
Psalm 63:1, 6–8 (NIV)

A year had passed since Brion, my husband, died. My heart was still profoundly broken. One night, grief overwhelmed me. My Bible was beside me, but almost defiantly I pointed to the empty pillow, 'God, I don't want to read my Bible! I want to see Brion's face. That's what I want!' At first I was shocked by my own words, and then I felt refreshed with the strong sense that God was hearing my cry. A sense of peace filled me.

Eventually, I opened my Bible to Psalm 63. King David's own son Absalom had betrayed him and threatened his kingdom. David's words of lament became my own. Amid my overwhelming sorrow, I understood that God's nearness was all I needed. God was present. His indescribable presence seemed to sit beside me, bringing comfort.

I have learned that God meets us in those desert places of brokenness—the time of our greatest need. I have found him to be enough and very near. I no longer feel alone. Instead, I am protected by God's perfect love.

Prayer: *God of all comfort, thank you for seeing our need and hearing our cries. Help us to cling to you always. Amen*

Thought for the day: God hears the cry of my deepest loss.

Laurie LaCross (California, US)

Perspectives

Read Matthew 22:36–40

In the same way you judge others, you will be judged, and with the measure you use, it will be measured to you.
Matthew 7:2 (NIV)

The way we see God affects the way we see ourselves. If we imagine God to be a demanding boss, we expect to be rewarded or punished based on our performance. But if we believe that he is a loving father, we see ourselves as children—imperfect, yet adored.

Focusing on our flaws, faults and failures can lead us to see the same imperfections in others. When we are unkind, impatient and irritable toward others, it's often because we treat ourselves the same way. If we have trouble forgiving ourselves, we may also tend to hang on to the wrongs others have done to us.

Recently I looked in the mirror and saw a man I didn't like, a man who wasn't always polite or friendly. But God didn't see what I saw. As I stared at my reflection, I felt God whisper, 'You should speak to that man in the mirror gently and pray for him with compassion. You should love that man—because I do.'

God doesn't ignore our sins; he forgives us. And we can do the same—for ourselves and for others.

Prayer: *Dear Father, help us see what you see and do what you do. Amen*

Thought for the day: Because God loves me, I can love myself.

Jeff Adams (Arizona, US)

The Perfect Gift of Love

Read John 14:15–20

Jesus said, 'Peace I leave with you; my peace I give you. I do not give to you as the world gives. Do not let your hearts be troubled and do not be afraid.'

John 14:27 (NIV)

When my grandparents retired and decided to move into a smaller home, they asked family members to come and choose some special mementoes from the items they couldn't take with them. One of the items I chose was a colourful dish. The curved bowl had no great monetary value, but it holds special memories for me. Whenever we went to visit, the dish was always filled with small sweets. Each grandchild was invited to take a few. That was Grandma's way of letting us know we were special and welcome in her home. When I look at that dish, I am reminded of her love for me.

God also considers each of us special and has an abundance of gifts and blessings to give us. His blessings come to us in many different ways if we are open to receiving them. They come as the gift of a friend who lends a listening ear, the beauty of a new flower in bloom, or the many second chances God offers. God is a perfect parent who showers us with love. He is always ready to hear from us and forgive us when we come with an open heart.

Prayer: *Dear God, thank you for the gift of eternal life paid for by the death of your Son and our Lord Jesus. Amen*

Thought for the day: Today I will give thanks for the many blessings God has given me.

Christine Henderson (Texas, US)

Joy in Times of Stress

Read Psalm 118:21–24

This is the day that the Lord has made; let us rejoice and be glad in it.
Psalm 118:24 (NRSV)

My husband and I were going through some difficult times with work-related stress and financial worries. We had moved back to the United States after living in another country. We accepted the first jobs we were offered and pinching pennies became a way of life as we struggled to pay our bills on our new incomes. The need to find better employment overshadowed our lives. The stress made it difficult to enjoy life, and over time it began to wear on us.

One morning as I was meditating, the verse quoted above came to my mind. For the first time in a while, I thought about joys that I could find in the world every day. I remembered that a walk in the woods had brought me close to the fresh scent of trees and soil, the musical sound of birds conversing and the feeling of a gentle breeze across my face. And it didn't cost a penny!

Scripture helped me to realise that every day can bring something to enjoy, if I will only look for it. In time my husband and I got back into the habit of seeing God's gifts right in front of us, and that went a long way toward easing our stress. The Lord has created within this day and every day many reasons to rejoice and be glad.

Prayer: *Loving Father, help us to allow the joy of your world to reach us even during times of stress. Amen*

Thought for the day: God made today, and that is a reason to rejoice!

Courtney Hill Gulbro (Alabama, US)

Full of Life Again

Read Luke 15:11–20
He ran to his son, threw his arms around him and kissed him.
Luke 15:20 (NIV)

In our HIV/AIDS clinic, we maintain a rose garden to honour the patients we serve. We grow red roses as a sign of love and solidarity, and white roses in memory of those who have died from this pandemic disease.

One day I found, to my dismay, that someone had walked through the garden and carelessly trampled two rose bushes. As I looked at the scene, I saw one terribly damaged white rose with some buds lying in the mud. I picked it up, filled a glass jar with water, and placed the lifeless rose in it. To my surprise, my small effort was enough! A few hours later, the rose and leaves were fully extended, the buds had opened up and its full beauty was on display.

The lesson in this for me is that no matter in what condition God finds us, we can rest assured that he will embrace us and attend to us lovingly. Through our small acts of compassion, we can find a new sense of purpose so that we can flourish and let the beauty of God's love show through us.

Prayer: *Gracious God, thank you for creating us anew. Help us to shine your love into a world so desperately in need of it. Amen*

Thought for the day: No life is too broken for God to make it new.

Pascual P. Torres (Cortés, Honduras)

Just Like My Father

Read John 14:8–14

Let your light so shine before men, that they may see your good works, and glorify your Father which is in heaven.
Matthew 5:16 (KJV)

For as long as I can remember, I wanted to be just like my dad. He was my hero and my best friend. I loved everything Dad loved. I loved fishing, window shopping (especially at the sports shop and the hardware shop), and target shooting with my bow and arrow or rifle. If it was what my dad loved to do, I did too. I loved horses, Stetson hats and my country. I wanted to be a Marine when I grew up, just like my dad.

Just as I wanted to be like my dad when I was a child, as an adult, I want to be like my heavenly Father. I want to strive to love others as God loves, unconditionally and sacrificially, and to forgive others as God has always graciously forgiven me. I want to bring light into dark places, joy into places of sadness and healing into places of pain.

With the power given us by the Holy Spirit, we can be like the Father and like the Son. We can make a difference in our world as we follow Christ.

Prayer: *Dear God, may we be more like you with each passing day so that others will come to know your love and grace. In the name of Jesus Christ our Lord. Amen*

Thought for the day: I can strive to be like my heavenly Father and make a difference in the world.

Belinda Jo 'B.J.' Mathias (Mississippi, US)

Calmed Storms

Read Mark 4:35–41

I am convinced that neither death, nor life… nor height, nor depth, nor anything else in all creation, will be able to separate us from the love of God in Christ Jesus our Lord.
Romans 8:38–39 (NRSV)

In today's reading, the disciples were overcome by fear and woke Jesus from a sound sleep. They cried out and questioned his care for them. He calmed the wind and waves with the command, 'Peace! Be still!' Jesus then challenged the disciples, 'Why are you afraid? Have you still no faith?'

Similarly, the storms of life assault us with little or no warning. Winds of change scream and howl. We are tossed up on the shore like driftwood, where we may find ourselves lying among the wreckage of serious health problems, ruptured family relationships or broken dreams.

When we face hard times, grief and pain can dominate our days and fear may visit us in the middle of the night. Like the disciples, we cry out, 'Lord, do you not care that we are perishing?' Jesus may not instantly command these winds and waves, 'Be still!' But he does say to us, 'Peace!' He speaks with loving-kindness to comfort and strengthen us.

Scripture reminds us that our Lord will never leave us or forsake us. We are encouraged to cast all our cares, concerns, hurts, fears and pain on God because he cares for us (see 1 Peter 5:7).

Prayer: *Thank you, Lord, for hearing our prayers and giving us your peace in the stormy times of our lives. Amen*

Thought for the day: Jesus gives me peace during the storms of life.

Patricia Wilgis-Patton (Texas, US)

Stranded in the Desert

Read Matthew 6:5–8

The Lord says, 'Before they call I will answer; while they are still speaking I will hear.'
Isaiah 65:24 (NIV)

While on a two-year trip around the world in a Volkswagen campervan, I was stranded in the Sahara Desert for several days. The Hoggar, the track I was following through Algeria across the Sahara, is deeply corrugated. Driving on it is like driving on railway tracks. The punishing roadway caused two shock absorbers in the campervan to explode simultaneously, breaking the chassis.

After waiting for three days, I saw a traveller pull up behind me in a small van. On the roof of his vehicle, he had a complete set of welding equipment. Unfortunately, neither the traveller nor I knew how to weld, and he had no welding rod. I prayed and then remembered the steel coat hangers I had packed away. With torch and coat hanger in hand, I climbed under the campervan and somehow managed to weld the broken piece back onto the car.

I discovered that the man with the welding outfit had started his trip into the desert long after I had but before my crisis had occurred. This reminded me of the words of the Lord quoted above.

We never know what the future holds or what crises or difficulties might lie in front of us. But by faith, we can know that God is always present. In fact, his answer is on the way even before we call.

Prayer: *Dear Lord, we may not understand what is happening to us now or what we might face in the future, but help us to turn to you for the answers. Amen*

Thought for the day: No matter what difficulty I face, God is in it with me.

Randy Swanson (Utah, US)

Just Help

Read Matthew 7:9–12

Jesus said, 'Don't judge, so that you won't be judged. You'll receive the same judgement you give. Whatever you deal out will be dealt out to you.'
Matthew 7:1–2 (CEB)

My wife and I were enjoying our drive together when we passed a man holding a sign that read, 'Will Work for Food'. Later, we saw him getting into a car. Cynically, I wondered aloud what he was going to do with the money. But my wife asked me to follow him so we could give him some money anyway.

He pulled into a petrol station and bought only a tiny amount of petrol. My wife and I quickly agreed that I should talk with him. He indicated that he had lost his job, had not been able to find work for over six months, and that he was trying to feed his family. I told him that we would like to help him in the name of Christ.

While I filled his car with petrol, my wife went with the man and bought some food for his family. As we parted, my wife and I gave him more money and a copy of *The Upper Room*, and we said a prayer together.

Through my wife, God taught me a lesson. Since that day I've been less judgemental and more accepting of others. How that man used the gifts we gave him was between him and God. I learned that it is not my place to judge but to help.

Prayer: *Dear God, thank you for teaching us to care for others and to leave any judgement of others to you. In the name of Jesus we pray. Amen*

Thought for the day: My Christian faith frees me to give without judgement.

Albert Brooks Drake, Jr (Indiana, US)

God is Near

Read Psalm 34:1–7

The Lord is close to the broken-hearted and saves those who are crushed in spirit.
Psalm 34:18 (NIV)

Reading my evening passage of scripture, I was turning the verses into prayer, but as I came to verse 18 of Psalm 34 I felt the tears welling up. God doesn't take away the pain of bereavement, but he is near to us, and does give us peace and joy as he has promised. He gives us the courage to face life without our loved one, but even so, some days the loneliness is hard to bear.

Then I remembered I was expecting a phone call. I am so grateful for the telephone, and God has given me a new ministry to other widows.

My friend phoned and we talked about the way God speaks to us through the words of scripture. We shared our sorrows and our joys, and prayed together, knowing that the Lord hears and was answering us in his own way and time.

Bereavement of any kind is painful, but God can and will turn it to good. We can keep on the lookout for new doors of opportunity he opens for us, and best of all find that he is drawing us into a closer relationship with himself.

Prayer: *Dear Lord, thank you for being with us during our times of bereavement. Help us to remember that nothing can separate us from your love. Amen*

Thought for the day: God is our hope in difficult times.

Pauline Lewis (South Glamorgan, Wales)

Respond With Love

Read Luke 6:27–31

Bless those who curse you. Pray for those who mistreat you.
Luke 6:28 (CEB)

Years ago I worked with individuals who had suffered traumatic brain injuries. Most of my clients were people who had been in motorcycle or car accidents. Some of them were able to interact with staff and others who had similar injuries. Others were prisoners in their own bodies.

It was my job to help each person to become as independent as they could. I assisted each person with eating meals, completing light work and playing table games. Their injuries made many of my clients susceptible to sudden outbursts of anger and sometimes violence. Any staff member on the receiving end of an outburst was trained not to take it personally—it was only a symptom of the brain injury. We were trained to remain calm and ignore the outburst. I wondered whether I could apply this knowledge to the rest of my life.

In today's reading, Jesus teaches us to turn the other cheek to outbursts from others. People may act out because of a traumatic event or situation in their lives. If we don't take these outbursts personally, we can follow Jesus' instruction and respond with love.

Prayer: *Dear God, help us to respond with your love when others act out of their pain. Amen*

Thought for the day: How can I respond with God's love to outbursts of anger?

Scott Wierenga (Michigan, US)

Supplying Our Needs

Read Matthew 6:25–34

[God] who supplies seed to the sower and bread for food will supply and multiply your seed for sowing and increase the harvest of your righteousness.
2 Corinthians 9:10 (NRSV)

The young ministers in my denomination faced a financial crisis during our ministries in the 1990s. For a few months, we did not receive our monthly payments. We were told that auditors were examining the accounts because of some irregularities.

Since most of us and our spouses were dependent upon the meagre church income, we had great difficulty providing for our families' daily needs. I thank God that during those days none of us left our place of ministry; in fact, our ministries became more effective. The businesses in our area gave us provisions to sustain us. We all found assurance in the words of Matthew 6:33: 'Seek ye first the kingdom of God, and his righteousness; and all these things shall be added unto you.'

It was a big challenge for us to look after the parish work and to maintain our families at the same time. But Jesus promised rest saying, 'Take my yoke upon you, and learn from me; for I am gentle and humble in heart, and you will find rest for your souls' (Matthew 11:29). And we can trust Christ to fulfil this promise.

Prayer: *Loving Saviour and Sustainer, thank you for responding to our needs through our communities and for granting us rest. In Jesus' name. Amen*

Thought for the day: When I seek to do God's will, I can find purpose and rest.

Benjamin R.K. Lall (Assam, India)

A Safe Place

Read Psalm 91:1–4

The peace of God, which surpasses all understanding, will guard your hearts and your minds in Christ Jesus.
Philippians 4:7 (NRSV)

When I was a young girl, at times I found my home to be a frightening place because my mother was an alcoholic. I often sought refuge outside in the large lilac bushes that grew behind our house. Their dense, leaf-covered branches stretched high before bending over toward the ground. At the base of the bushes, among their trunks and shoots, was a small open space where I could hide. My hiding place was dark, but I could see the bright sunlight through the branches. No one could see me. Beneath the lilac bushes was my safe place, where I felt protected.

As an adult, I sometimes find the world to be a frightening place. The news is full of terrible tragedies: earthquakes, floods, fires, epidemics, terrorist acts, senseless killings, financial collapses. However, I no longer need to find a physical hiding place where I can somehow escape from the world. Through Jesus Christ, I've been blessed with the 'peace of God, which surpasses all understanding'.

Jesus assured us that he would be with us no matter where we are or what we experience. Christ loves us. He is our safe place.

Prayer: *Dear Lord, when the problems and trials of the world overwhelm us, remind us of your faithfulness. Help us to trust you. Amen*

Thought for the day: True peace comes from God.

Marilou Reed (Florida, US)

Finish It

Read Genesis 2:1–3

The hands of Zerubbabel have laid the foundation of this house; his hands shall also finish it; and thou shalt know that the Lord of hosts hath sent me unto you.
Zechariah 4:9 (KJV)

I recently got a new job at an agricultural research centre. When I first started, the job was challenging, and my motivation was low because it was a new field of work for me. The requirements for promotion include writing and publishing research papers.

On many occasions, I have started a research project only to stop halfway through. As I constantly abandoned my work I wondered if I would ever be able to earn promotion.

One Sunday as I sat in the pew during a church service my minister read today's scripture verse, and I felt something fire up within me. My renewed passion was so great that it sustained me until the end of the research project I was working on at the time.

Many of us have projects we have left incomplete, dreams we have abandoned and aspirations that have waned. But the words of Zechariah still ring true for us today. With God's help, we can finish the work we have started.

Prayer: *Dear Father, help us to finish the works of our hands by your grace. May we never leave undone the work you have given to us. Amen*

Thought for the day: God has given me work to do and, with his help, I will finish it.

Nwakuche Emeka (Nigeria)

God's Gift

Read Ecclesiastes 5:18–20

May the righteous be glad and rejoice before God; may they be happy and joyful.
Psalm 68:3 (NIV)

When I was younger, I would notice wealthy friends and how happy they seemed. I had difficulty understanding why I didn't have the same privileges as my friends. But then another friend said to me, 'I don't know why people are so unhappy when every day is a gift.' My friend was right. Every day is a gift.

As I have matured, I have learned from the Bible about the gift of joy and the simple values that bring happiness. Why do I worry about what I don't have when life is an opportunity to make the most of what God gives? Delighting in what God calls us to do brings us true joy. The gift of waking up in the morning, seeing a new day with new opportunities, and knowing that all of our many blessings come from God's grace and mercy can bring deep happiness.

Now when I wake up, I look at what is there in front of me and I don't think about the things which I don't have. Every hour, minute and second bring an opportunity to make a difference. I have learned that trying to take control of my life often results in disappointment, but allowing God to be my leader is a rewarding spiritual experience.

Prayer: *Dear God, open our eyes so that we can see and appreciate all you have given to us. Amen*

Thought for the day: I will be grateful and celebrate God's gift of life today.

Courtney Pack (Georgia, US)

Letting Go

Read Matthew 11:28–30

Do not worry about anything, but in everything by prayer and supplication with thanksgiving let your requests be made known to God.
Philippians 4:6 (NRSV)

In coastal Louisiana, one popular way we catch blue crab is to tie a piece of meat onto a long piece of string and throw the bait out from the shore. When we feel a crab tugging on the bait, we slowly start pulling the line the 15 or 20 feet to the bank. The crabs tenaciously hold on to the bait until they are dragged over a net in the shallow water and scooped up. This method works consistently, because the crabs don't know when it is in their best interest to let go.

People can be like that too. Holding onto something—especially a heavy burden—requires as much effort as the crabs bumping along the bottom of the ocean.

As humans, sometimes we hold onto our problems by trying to solve them ourselves. We don't look at the big picture and we forget the wisdom of letting go. Scripture tells us to acknowledge our powerlessness and fully turn over our problems to God, but to be able to do that we have to be willing to let go of them. It is then that God sends us the peace that surpasses all understanding and guides us through our crisis.

Prayer: *Dear Lord, help us to trust that it is better for us to put our problems in your hands than to keep them in ours. Amen*

Thought for the day: What problem can I turn over to God today?

David McCain (Louisiana, US)

One Family

Read Psalm 65:2–8

You who answer prayer, to you all people will come.
Psalm 65:2 (NIV)

As a Spanish teacher, I have had the opportunity to meet people from many countries, cultures and religions over the years. God has blessed me in these encounters.

One of the loveliest experiences I have had was in Puerto Rico with a young Christian woman from Indonesia. This young woman was far from her family and felt lonely in Puerto Rico. No one in our area spoke her native language. However, she and I both spoke English, so we could communicate while she learned Spanish.

When we prayed, she prayed in her language and I in mine. Together we opened our hearts—praying and crying to God—united in our willingness to be attentive to the presence of the Holy Spirit. We remain grateful that God not only listens to our prayers but understands our common needs.

Prayer: *God of all, thank you for the privilege of praying for and with one another regardless of our differences. We pray as Jesus taught us, saying, 'Our Father which art in heaven, Hallowed be thy name. Thy kingdom come. Thy will be done, in earth as it is in heaven. Give us this day our daily bread. And forgive us our debts, as we forgive our debtors. And lead us not into temptation, but deliver us from evil. For thine is the kingdom, and the power, and the glory, for ever.'* Amen*

Thought for the day: The Holy Spirit unites us as one family.

Aida I. Rojas (Puerto Rico)

PRAYER FOCUS: INTERNATIONAL STUDENTS AND TEACHERS
* Matthew 6:9–13 (KJV)

'It's Official!'

Read Romans 8:10–17
Those who are led by the Spirit of God are the children of God.
Romans 8:14 (NIV)

On the day our request for adoption was granted, our family and friends filled the judge's chambers to capacity. Our beautiful daughter listened attentively as the judge read the legal, binding decree of adoption. When the judge signed, stamped and granted the request for her adoption, our three-year-old daughter cried out, 'It's official!', and the room exploded in applause. Three months later we received a new birth certificate naming my husband and me as the parents—legal and binding, precisely the same as if we had given birth to her.

We loved and adored our daughter from the moment we saw her, but she was not legally our child until the adoption was complete. In the same way, God loved us before we were even born and made a way for us to become adopted children through faith in Jesus.

Our adoption as children of God was made possible the moment Jesus cried out on the cross, 'It is finished!' Now all who accept Christ's gift of saving love and willingly follow him will be adopted and treated in all respects as God's own children. Through adoption, we become brothers and sisters in Christ and receive the love and peace that God provides.

Prayer: *Thank you, Abba, Father, for making us your very own children through the sacrifice of your Son, Jesus, in whose name we pray. Amen*

Thought for the day: We are God's forever children.

Michele M. Rizzo (California, US)

The Good Samaritan

'Who is my neighbour?' Jesus responds to the lawyer's question with a story about a man travelling on the Jericho road who was robbed, stripped naked, beaten and left for dead. In his helplessness he was passed by twice—first by a priest and then a Levite—who crossed to the other side of the road to avoid the man.

The road between Jerusalem and Jericho was widely known to be dangerous. Travelling along it was potentially hazardous, and halting one's journey for any length of time courted serious risk. The priest and Levite may have weighed this risk in their minds and decided that the increased threat to their safety wasn't worth it. It's easy for me to shake my finger at them both. Shame on you priest and Levite! But I can't shake my finger long before I feel the pangs of hypocrisy.

I too am guilty of their choice. I have done what I could to avoid someone in need of help, and I can imagine what the priest and Levite might have thought: 'I have somewhere to be' or 'Someone else will offer help' or 'I do a lot for other people.' I do not know what grief they felt—if any—at having left the man for dead. What I do know is that neither the priest nor the Levite did anything; it was a Samaritan who took action.

By all accounts, the priest and the Levite were the ones most likely to help the man. I have to wrestle with the fact that it was a Samaritan—an outsider, foreigner and unlikely character—who bandaged the man's wounds, put him on the Samaritan's own donkey and found him somewhere to stay.

I generally think I am a neighbour to someone when I make them a cake or water their plants while they are on holiday, and someone is a neighbour to me when they do the same. Of course, these are good and decent things to do for each other. But if I pay close attention to the parable, I come away from it uncomfortable about what it asks of me. Being a neighbour is about more than making a cake or watering plants. These are things I would do for people I am likely to help, people who are likely to do something for me in return. But what about the people I am unlikely to help, the people no one expects me to help? What about those I will walk around to avoid?

As I study this parable, I am beginning to understand that Jesus is calling me to act with unguarded compassion toward someone unlikely—the person who doesn't look like me, speak like me or have the same customs and ideas as I have. The good Samaritan reminds me that being a neighbour to someone may involve risking my comfort, my own concerns and priorities, or my time and commitments. It reminds me of the times I have passed someone in need; and if I take the story seriously, I can no longer leave someone 'lying on the side of the road'. It also reminds me that the next time I find myself in dire straits, it could be the most unlikely person who stops to help.

Several meditations in this issue address our responsibility as Christians to help those in need. You may want to read again the meditations for July 1, 15, 17 and 19 and August 1, 6, 18, 23, 26 and 29, before responding to the reflection questions below.

Questions for Reflection:

1. Read Luke 10:30–37. Which character in the parable of the good Samaritan do you identify with most closely? Why?

2. Can you recall a time when you saw someone in need of help but passed them by? What was the situation? What did you learn from the experience? What will you do differently if you find yourself in a similar situation in the future?

Andrew Garland Breeden
Associate/Acquisitions Editor

A Small Part?

Read 1 Corinthians 12:12–25

There are many parts, but one body. The eye cannot say to the hand, 'I don't need you!' And the head cannot say to the feet, 'I don't need you!' On the contrary, those parts of the body that seem to be weaker are indispensable.
1 Corinthians 12:20–22 (NIV)

I work on an assembly line making car mirrors. When building my designated part at my station, I sometimes get frustrated at how insignificant my role seems. But then I remind myself that if I don't do my job right and time it well with the people on either side of me, then the whole process can fail. I also have to acknowledge that mirrors serve an important purpose for drivers.

In our Christian service, we may also devalue our role. But, for example, helping people feel welcome in church can influence them for God in ways we may never fully understand. God can express love and care in myriad ways, but we are his hands and feet in the world. One of the privileges of being members of the body of Christ is ministering to one another and to those outside the church. Though we may not see the end results of our small tasks, God sees how our small part in the body of Christ helps further the gospel in the lives of those around us and in the world.

Prayer: *Dear God, thank you for allowing us to be part of such a diverse body and empowering us to serve. Amen*

Thought for the day: God can help me use every skill I have to serve others.

Keith Osmun (Ohio, US)

What Really Matters

Read Proverbs 3:13–18

Thus says the Lord God, See, I am laying in Zion a foundation stone, a tested stone, a precious cornerstone, a sure foundation: 'One who trusts will not panic.'
Isaiah 28:16 (NRSV)

After many years, my wife and I had reached the point when we could no longer care for our home. The family we had raised was grown and gone, and our years of working were at an end. What had once been a 'labour of love' had just become a 'labour'. It was time to move on.

Moving is never easy, but it's even harder when you know that so much of what you've gathered and cherished for so long must be left behind for ever. We prayed that God would help us decide what we could not decide on our own.

Then I remembered all the wonderful stories throughout the Bible, powerful tales of men and women who gave up every possession they owned and placed their trust in God's wisdom alone. Knowing that God loves us always and will never lead us astray made taking the first hard step toward moving much easier. My wife and I now know that regardless of the earthly things we give up, seeking God's will and obeying it is all that really matters.

Prayer: *Dear God, never let us forget that as long as we are with you, we have not lost everything. Amen*

Thought for the day: When we are with God, we are always at home.

Mark A. Carter (Texas, US)

Learning to Walk Again

Read Isaiah 40:27–31

Though we stumble, we shall not fall headlong, for the Lord holds us by the hand.
Psalm 37:24 (NRSV)

My recovery from hip surgery includes intensive daily physical therapy to retrain the muscles in my weakened leg. I begin with gentle massage and then progress to active muscle-strengthening exercises. Finally, I advance to the treadmill, gripping the handrails firmly, lest I stumble while my legs recall how to walk correctly. Daily therapy takes time and effort, but it's worth it. I feel a little stronger each day.

I'm learning that I need the same discipline in my spiritual walk. Limping along is easy for me. I skip daily devotions when time is short and pray only briefly while rushing from one activity to another. Over time, my spiritual muscles weaken until I am no longer able to walk with confidence through the challenges of daily life. However, through prayer, devotional reading, Bible study and worship I am able to strengthen my walk with God. When difficulties arise and I stumble, God is holding my hand, lifting me up and offering me the opportunity to renew my spiritual journey.

Prayer: *Dear Lord, thank you for being with us through the challenges of life. Please strengthen our desire to walk more closely with you. Amen*

Thought for the day: When we stumble, God is there to catch us and give us strength.

Susan Walker-Spring (New York, US)

The Bread of Life

Read John 6:35–40

[Jesus said] 'I am the living bread that came down from heaven.'
John 6:51 (NIV)

Encouraged after watching 'The Great British Bake Off', I began making my bread from scratch. After years of using a bread-making machine, it was quite a long job as I measured the ingredients and added them one by one to a bowl, then kneaded and proved the mixture. After more kneading and proving the dough was ready to put into the oven. And the result? Wonderful, even if I do say so myself!

On reflection I thought that the process of making my bread could be likened to our Christian walk.

When we open our hearts to Jesus he meets us where we are and begins the process of bringing 'ingredients' together in our life: new friendships, a new church, reading the Bible, prayer and worship. These he uses together to remould what may seem to us our messy lives. Over time the process can be daunting and challenging and even painful—much as my dough had to be pummelled, proved and placed in a hot oven. However, by allowing the 'ingredients' to take hold, our new structure and new way of living will eventually seem right to us, and we will one day be changed into the person God intends us to be. All we experience will, in God's hands, bring us into a new relationship with him and with others.

Prayer: *Thank you, Lord, that you love us so much. Transform us, we pray, into the people you intend us to be. Amen*

Thought for the day: God is moulding me day by day into a new person.

Linda Cunningham (Middlesex, England)

Answer to Prayer

Read Acts 8:26–38

An angel of the Lord said to Philip, 'Go south to the road—the desert road—that goes down from Jerusalem to Gaza.' So he started out, and on his way he met an Ethiopian eunuch.
Acts 8:26–27 (NIV)

I could smell the paint drying on my latest work as I knelt to pray, 'Thank you, God, for inspiring me to do this piece. Now whom do you want me to give it to?' God brought my sister to mind, but I said, 'Lord, she's an atheist.' My sister would roll her eyes whenever anyone spoke about religion. However, I obeyed God's nudging, even enclosing a note explaining that God had told me to send the painting to her.

Weeks later I received her response: 'I was praying to God for a sign—then I got this piece from you not even an hour later. When I read that God told you it was for me, I cried. I have opened my heart to him.'

My sister may think I was the answer to her prayer, but really she was the answer to mine. God helped our prayers to intersect at a critical juncture that changed both our lives for the better.

Being in prison on death row, I often question how and why God would possibly use me. I struggle with feelings of worthlessness, despite being a sincere, repentant believer and despite the Bible's saying God has a plan for each of us. My sister's letter affirmed to me that God can work through every member of the body of Christ, including me and my sister.

Prayer: *Dear God, give us the faith to obey your Spirit, even when we don't know or understand what you're trying to accomplish. Amen*

Thought for the day: Today I will pay attention to where God is leading me.

George T. Wilkerson (North Carolina, US)

Always Prepared

Read Matthew 25:1–13
Keep watch, because you do not know the day or the hour.
Matthew 25:13 (NIV)

As kitchen staff, we have a responsibility to keep our workplace clean. Every day before we leave for home, my colleagues and I clean the work surfaces and cooking utensils, scrub the floor and wipe the tables in the dining room. Keeping the workplace clean is important because it protects people's health. We could also get into trouble with the public health department if we ignored their requirements. Someone from that office inspects our premises frequently, but we never know when the person is coming. That's why we always do our cleaning daily.

Our need for diligence reminds me of the second coming of Jesus. Our scripture verse for today encourages us to keep watch. Like the five wise virgins who took extra oil for their lamps, we must be constantly prepared for our Lord to come again. Unwavering faith in God and obedience to his commands will keep us ready to welcome Jesus when he comes again. And at that time, I want to be among those who are ready to receive him and to enter into his eternal kingdom.

Prayer: *O God, help us walk in your path day by day until the time Christ comes again. In Jesus' name we pray. Amen*

Thought for the day: How prepared am I to receive Jesus when he comes again?

Amy Sutikdja (North Rhine-Westphalia, Germany)

Strong Roots

Read John 15:1–10

Continue to live your lives in [Christ Jesus], rooted and built up in him and established in the faith, just as you were taught, abounding in thanksgiving.
Colossians 2:6–7 (NRSV)

My daily walk goes by a lake that has cypress trees along the banks. One day I stopped to look more closely at one of these trees and its large, entangled roots. Some of the roots were wound tightly around the tree; others grew out from the tree. Still other roots seemed to sprout from the trunk of the tree itself. Many seemed tangled together. I marvelled at the tree's strong root system.

I thought about how much our life with God is like this tree. We, too, need the support of strong roots. Some of the roots grow straight and tall, mimicking the strong and direct teachings from scripture and the church. Others wrap around one another, forming strong support groups of friends and family, which encircle us and hold us tight with love. And others extend away from the tree, reminding us that we are to reach out and embrace others with God's great love. I keep this image of the strong root system of the cypress tree as a guide to live by, knowing that I need many types of support to stay strong and connected to God.

Prayer: *Holy God, help us to remember that we are connected to you and our community of faith just as strong roots are connected to a tree. Amen*

Thought for the day: Today I will stay rooted in God's love.

Patricia M. Daniels (Florida, US)

Sharing My Faith

Read 1 Peter 3:13–16

Make up your mind not to worry beforehand how you will defend yourselves. For I will give you words and wisdom that none of your adversaries will be able to resist or contradict.
Luke 21:14–15 (NIV)

While I was studying as an exchange student in Japan, I was out of my comfort zone. Life was difficult. Once, a friend invited me to a birthday dinner where I did not know any of the other three guests. Thankfully, since we were all students at the same university, we had some things in common to talk about while we ate pizza and pasta.

Then one of the women asked me, 'What is your religion?' I responded, 'I am a Christian.' She and the other woman asked me about the importance of religion, what I believed, and even about politics and the global financial crisis. The other man started asking about the core tenets of my denomination. To cap it all off, he asked about the Holy Trinity! After two hours of conversation I learned that my three new friends all belong to other religions, but they said that they had come to understand Christianity better.

On my way back to my room, I asked myself if I had spoken the truth. Did I show that my relationship with Christ is the centre of my life? Did I help others to see that love is the focus and the essence of my faith? Today's verse gave me peace. As long as we keep our relationship with Christ, we can trust God to help us to say and do the right things at the right time.

Prayer: *Dear Lord, help us to glorify you through all that we say and do so that other people come to know you. Amen*

Thought for the day: God can help me share my faith in any situation.

Richard Mel Caplis (Benguet, Philippines)

Daily Praise

Read Psalm 103:1–5
This is the day that the Lord has made; let us rejoice and be glad in it.
Psalm 118:24 (NRSV)

Life can be busy, with endless responsibilities. I get caught up in the chaos and stress of today's fast-paced lifestyle. By day's end I am often tense, exhausted and impatient.

Lately, when I put my three-year-old to bed, he says to me, 'Mummy, I think it's going to be a beautiful day tomorrow.' This simple statement has affected me profoundly. His words remind me that each day is a gift from God, full of beauty and blessings. Now, instead of fretting over what I didn't accomplish that day and worrying about tomorrow, I reflect on the blessings I have received. I try to recognise the beauty all around me and look forward to what God has in store while offering a prayer of thanksgiving. I am more focused on God's grace, and I can see his work in my life and in the world more clearly.

My children and I now greet each morning by reciting Psalm 118:24 together, and I repeat it throughout the day when I find myself becoming anxious or overwhelmed. Now, even in the midst of life's busyness and complexities, I am able to proclaim like the psalmist, 'Let my whole being bless the Lord and never forget all his good deeds' (Psalm 103:2, CEB).

Prayer: *Gracious God, thank you for your many blessings. Help us to let go of stress and remain full of adoration and gratitude to you. Amen*

Thought for the day: I will praise God for the beauty and blessings of each day.

Julie Calleja (Michigan, US)

Faith and Praise

Read Luke 6:12–19

During those days [Jesus] went out to the mountain to pray; and he spent the night in prayer to God.
Luke 6:12 (NRSV)

The red traffic light at the crossroads seemed to take for ever. I sat in my car, fuming impatiently, tapping my fingers on the steering wheel. I had a long list of errands.

Then it hit me. When else during the day will I have some quiet time to listen for what God is telling me? When else will I have time to remember in prayer those who are close to my heart? As I prayed, I calmed down, the light changed and I drove away. My green light had come in more ways than one.

Too often we are distracted by our to-do lists. Focusing on the here and now is often easier than looking to the hereafter. Even Jesus had some quiet time, and his 'list' was longer than mine. After spending his day healing and feeding the multitudes, he taught his disciples. In the midst of all that, he did the one thing necessary: he took the time to walk away from the crowds and to pray. Thinking of Jesus sitting quietly on a mountaintop helps me to control my impatience and reminds me to take advantage of unexpected quiet moments to pray.

Prayer: *Dear God, help us remember that all our time belongs to you. Amen*

Thought for the day: Prayer prepares me for the road ahead.

Patricia Marks (Georgia, US)

Letting Go of Life's Trophies

Read Romans 14:7–9

Teach us to count our days that we may gain a wise heart.
Psalm 90:12 (NRSV)

A hymn entitled 'The Old Rugged Cross' has this line in its chorus: 'I'll cherish the old rugged cross, till my trophies at last I lay down'. It is about the Christian hope of heaven, where we will lay aside our earthly trophies and receive a heavenly crown.

In my mid-eighties, I find myself grieving the 'trophies' of life that I have given up since I retired. As a retired minister, I seldom preach anymore. I also can no longer take part in sport and recreation that I once enjoyed, such as volleyball, swimming and leading canoe trips in the wilderness. For over 60 years one of my prized 'trophies' was my pilot's licence that enabled me to experience the joy of flight in a single-engine aircraft.

As I have meditated on the meaning of 'clinging to the old rugged cross', I have realised more clearly that I have no need to give up God's great redeeming love that comes to us through the life, death and resurrection of Jesus. My bodily aches and limitations do not hinder my participation in a life of faith. I give thanks for all that the cross of Christ means, and I commend that story of God's grace and goodness to all as the real transforming crown of this life and the life to come.

Prayer: *Dear Lord, regardless of our age or abilities, we want to be your faithful servants. Help us to keep Christ at the centre of our lives. Amen*

Thought for the day: The greatest trophy is God's sustaining love.

Elmer A. Dickson (Florida, US)

Mini-Miracles

Read John 2:1–11

Jesus did many other things as well. If every one of them were written down, I suppose that even the whole world would not have room for the books that would be written.
John 21:25 (NIV)

You would expect the Son of God to begin his ministry with a spectacular miracle: raising someone from the dead, multiplying loaves and fishes or at least walking on the sea. But Jesus launched his ministry by saving a party. More guests had shown up at a wedding reception than had sent in their RSVP cards, and now the punch bowl had run dry. So Jesus turned water into wine.

Turning water into wine doesn't bring anybody back from the dead, free anyone from a life-threatening illness or defy the forces of nature. It does, however, reveal a God who is interested not only in the life-and-death issues we face but also in our daily lives.

In the same way, the Lord works in even the mundane moments of our lives. A relationship with a God who was interested only in the big issues of life would not be a personal relationship. But our infinite, almighty God chooses to relate to us on a more intimate level—not only on the mountain tops but in the dining rooms of our lives.

Prayer: *Thank you, God, for the small miracles that show us how much you love and care for us. Amen*

Thought for the day: Where have I seen God's mini-miracles today?

James N. Watkins (Indiana, US)

Safely Back Home

Read Ezekiel 34:11–16

Which one of you, having a hundred sheep and losing one of them, does not leave the ninety-nine in the wilderness and go after the one that is lost until he finds it? When he has found it, he lays it on his shoulders and rejoices.

Luke 15:4–5 (NRSV)

I've always found jogging a good way to spend time with God. I have continued this practice during my work here in West Africa.

Because I am new to the area, it has taken me a while to become familiar both with my small village and the surrounding villages. Early one morning, during my third month of service, I went jogging. After some distance, I decided to turn back toward the village. With the sun rising on the horizon, I could see my way easily; but when I came to a fork in the road, I went the wrong way and ended up in an unfamiliar nearby village. At first anxiety overwhelmed me, but a local woman pointed me in the right direction. I walked for a while, but then realised I still wasn't sure where I was. Then, like a shepherd, a villager on a horse showed me to the junction that led toward my village.

As I was following my newfound 'shepherd,' I thought about our great shepherd who leads us home to God when we are lost.

Now I don't worry about getting lost, because I trust that Christ will lead me home every time.

Prayer: *Dear God, our Shepherd, when we become lost on our journey, seek us and lead us home to your loving embrace. Amen*

Thought for the day: God will always lead me home when I lose my way.

Ashley Justice (The Gambia)

God Travels

Read Deuteronomy 6:4–9

Come near to God, and he will come near to you.
James 4:8 (CEB)

Reading *The Upper Room* has become one of my early morning rituals. Before I do anything else, I read a daily meditation from the email that was sent to me in the middle of the night. Doing so helps me to clear my mind and prepare for the day.

However, I travel for work, sometimes across many time zones. The email containing the daily meditation arrives in my inbox at different points in the day. When I travel to the west coast of the United States, it arrives before I go to bed, becoming the last thing I read in the day. In China, it arrives shortly after lunch, leading me to pause in what I am doing to focus on the daily scripture and reflection. I have discovered that no time is the wrong time to pause for a moment with the Lord. No matter what the time or place, I read and contemplate God's word. Wherever we are and whatever we are doing, a conversation with God awaits. This is a tremendous blessing.

Prayer: *Dear God, thank you for transcending time and space to welcome us with your word. Amen*

Thought for the day: I can always make time to pause for God.

Andrew Billings (Alabama, US)

Live in Harmony

Read Romans 12:10–18
How good and pleasant it is when God's people live together in unity!
Psalm 133:1 (NIV)

I recently read a newspaper article about sociable weaver birds that live in the Kalahari Desert in Africa. They build nests large enough to house hundreds of birds on trees and other tall objects. The nests are used as shelter from the heat by day and the frigid temperatures of the desert by night.

The sociable weavers are hospitable and good hosts. They share their food and know how to work as a team, such as mending the nest when it shows signs of deterioration. They even allow a variety of other birds to live in their colonies. In this diverse setting, they live together in peace and harmony.

When I finished reading this interesting article, I concluded that the sociable weavers' behaviour is worthy of imitation within our families, churches and communities. This lesson from nature is also the lesson from today's reading. Paul reminds us that God calls us to love one another, to maintain our spiritual fervour, and to practise hospitality toward one another (see Romans 12:10–14).

Prayer: *Loving God, help us to live in harmony with our neighbours. Amen*

Thought for the day: 'Love your neighbour as yourself' (Matthew 22:39).

María M. Urdaz de Rosario (Puerto Rico)

Works of Art

Read Genesis 50:15–20

Joseph replied to his brothers, 'You intended to harm me, but God intended it for good to accomplish what is now being done, the saving of many lives.'
Genesis 50:20 (NIV)

A number of years ago I went for a walk in the woods with Bob, a friend from church who was a professor of forestry. As we were enjoying the natural surroundings, he showed me a basketball-sized, bulbous growth on the limb of a tree and told me it was a burr. The burr had created chaos in a tiny place, causing the tree to grow out of control, in any shape and every direction. As a result, the tree looked deformed and ugly to me. Yet Bob told me that woodworkers prize such growths because they make the most unique bowls and carvings. The grain is multicoloured, and it swirls in waves. Once polished, it becomes a unique work of art.

In much the same way that a skilled artist can turn a destructive force into a work of beauty, our loving God can turn our brokenness into unique works of grace and love.

Prayer: *Dear Father, work in the struggles of our lives to help us turn them into testimonies of your love and power, as we pray, 'Our Father in heaven, hallowed be your name, your kingdom come, your will be done, on earth as it is in heaven. Give us today our daily bread. And forgive us our debts, as we also have forgiven our debtors. And lead us not into temptation, but deliver us from the evil one.'* Amen*

Thought for the day: God can transform our brokenness into something beautiful.

Keith M. Curran (Virginia, US)

      * Matthew 6:9–13 (NIV)

Clothed in Kindness

Read Colossians 3:12–17

As God's chosen people, holy and dearly loved, clothe yourselves with compassion, kindness, humility, gentleness and patience.
Colossians 3:12 (NIV)

I was scared when we walked into A&E at 4 am. My husband had tingling and numbness down his left side and a slight limp, symptoms of a mini-stroke. As the staff showed us into a consulting room, I fought to hold back tears. I was anxious and afraid, but a nurse's kindness reassured me.

'My name is Sarah,' she said. 'You let me know if you need anything.' Sarah took a moment to smile and make eye contact with us. In fact, everyone who came into the room stopped to introduce themselves and ask if we were comfortable. With each smile, the hospital became less cold and scary. My fear subsided as I sensed God encouraging me through the quiet, friendly care of the staff.

What a difference kindness can make! It is a powerful way to share God's grace with others. When we put on kindness, we look more like Jesus. We never know when a thoughtful gesture could turn the day around for a colleague, a struggling child or the stranger behind us at the coffee shop. We can share the love of Christ with those around us through our kind words and actions.

Prayer: *Dear Lord, thank you for loving us. Help us to be like Christ, reaching out to others with kindness and compassion. Amen*

Thought for the day: Who might need to know Christ through my words or actions today?

Betsy de Cruz (Texas, US)

Saying 'Yes'

Read Judges 6:11–18

God did not give us a spirit of cowardice, but rather a spirit of power and of love and of self-discipline.

2 Timothy 1:7 (NRSV)

I was offered a new job with more responsibility and a substantial increase in salary. The job description was lengthy and intimidating. I began to feel anxious. It seemed to be a dream job, but I felt unprepared and under-qualified. I prayed, 'God, I just don't know about this.' I wrote to the company, explaining my concerns; and the next thing I knew, I had the job.

Scripture is filled with ordinary people called to do extraordinary things. The angel of the Lord called Gideon to deliver Israel from the Midianites. Gideon's response was something like this: 'My family is insignificant, and I am the most insignificant in my family' (Judges 6:15). Moses asked God to choose someone else to confront Pharaoh because he wasn't a public speaker (Exodus 4:10). And Saul hid in a baggage room on the day of his coronation (1 Samuel 10:22). God often selects the not-so-willing, and makes them capable.

At times, we all experience anxiety, feelings of inadequacy and doubt. But a renewed sense of God's presence within us gives us extraordinary abilities. When God calls us to take a job, to start a ministry, to extend a helping hand, we can rest assured that he also gives us the power, ability, love and self-discipline to accomplish the task.

Prayer: *Dear God, thank you for creating us to have an impact on the world. We ask your help as we take on new challenges. Amen*

Thought for the day: God gives me the courage to do new things.

Kenneth Avon White (Tennessee, US)

A Small World

Read Matthew 5:13–16

The King will reply [to those at his right hand], 'Truly I tell you, whatever you did for one of the least of these brothers and sisters of mine, you did for me.'
Matthew 25:40 (NIV)

As a child I was fascinated by maps. The world then seemed so big. Recently a charitable organisation sent me a map of the world, and I was struck by how small the world now seems. I am convinced that we cannot isolate ourselves when there is so much desperate need in the world.

I put the world map on my refrigerator and marked every place where I had made a donation: places recovering from a natural disaster, communities experiencing a health crisis, a refugee organisation for which I knitted gifts. I also include my own community where I have helped to fulfil a need. When friends travel abroad I give them a donation and ask them to share it wherever God nudges them. I do this so that this act will bless not only the one in need and me, but also my friend serving as an intermediary.

I believe that as citizens of the world we are called to make a difference with whatever we have and however we can. As the coloured arrows on my map have increased to include all the continents, I smile as I realise that even if I can't travel to all these areas I can still do something to help people there. I may never meet any of them, but I am certain that God is directing my resources to those who need my help.

Prayer: *Dear God of all, empower us to help those who are struggling in difficult situations beyond their control. Amen*

Thought for the day: I will follow God's nudge to help where I can.

Jeanne Carper (Maryland, US)

PRAYER FOCUS: THOSE LACKING THE NECESSITIES OF LIFE   89

A Simple Life

Read 1 Timothy 6:6–12

What does the Lord require of you but to do justice, and to love kindness, and to walk humbly with your God?
Micah 6:8 (NRSV)

My grandfather led a simple life; he was always content with whatever he received. He developed a good command of the English language as he worked with doctors and missionaries before and after India gained its independence.

When he retired, my grandfather dedicated his life to language and literature. He taught English to school children and college students. He wrote innumerable meditations and articles for Christian periodicals. He also wrote Christian books. His use of English helped to connect me to a wider cultural understanding.

At the age of 88, my grandfather died. It was evident from his funeral that he had had a powerful impact on the lives of those he encountered and had earned tremendous respect from our family and society. Through his simple lifestyle, he had used his talent with language to raise the Lord's name higher—adding joy and peace to other people's lives.

Our world often praises only those who dream big and achieve 'great' things. But then there are those who work in smaller ways with their God-given gifts to touch our lives and make them better. In today's restless world that's a challenge for us all.

Prayer: *Dear God, thank you for the people who have led us to you and have shown us how to live simply so that we can appreciate your blessings. Amen*

Thought for the day: Who has shown me how to live faithfully?

Rohan P. Diarsa (Gujarat, India)

Backward or Forward?

Read Ephesians 3:14–21

Jesus said, 'Unless a grain of wheat falls to the ground and dies, it remains only a single seed. But if it dies, it produces many seeds.'
John 12:24 (NIV)

Driving through a lush, green forest, I rounded a bend to see hundreds of white cylinders studding a bare hillside. The scene resembled a cemetery marked with rows of tombstones. Then I looked closer. Each white cylinder surrounded a tiny hand-planted sapling, protecting it from nibbling deer and harsh winds. In a few decades a forest would again cover this hill. I meditated on the larger truth of this picture: with loss comes space for new growth. Then I thought how often I have experienced the loss of possessions, people or jobs from my life. Each time, my immediate response was anger and frustration. I wasted energy looking backward when I could have been looking forward to the new life God could plant in that now-empty space.

Rather than fighting change, we can instead consider how much sooner something new and beautiful could grow if we would only hand over our pride and control to God, who longs to bless us. Contrary to the 'me first' attitude that the world encourages, God tells us that if we die to our selfish desires (see Galatians 5:24), we will see doors opening to new growth—'far more than all we can ask or imagine' (Ephesians 3:20).

Prayer: *Dear Lord, help us to trust you with our losses. Then help us to look forward to the new growth only you can provide. Amen*

Thought for the day: With each loss, God provides an opportunity for new growth.

Linda Jett (Oregon, US)

He's Been There

Read Hebrews 2:14–18; 4:14–16

Because [Jesus] himself suffered when he was tempted, he is able to help those who are being tempted.
Hebrews 2:18 (NIV)

When I was young and did something I shouldn't have, I knew I was about to get into trouble when my dad would come into my room, turn my chair around, and sit backwards on it. Once when the chair came out and I braced myself for a scolding, Dad said a few words that have stuck with me to this day. He said, 'Michael, when you think you've found a gutter I haven't crawled into, you let me know.' He was telling me two things: that he had been tempted by the same thing I had succumbed to, and also that I wasn't fooling him. Knowing this was unnerving, and yet it brought me closer to my father because I knew he could relate to me and that he cared for me.

Unlike my father and me, when faced with temptation, Jesus did not succumb to it (see Hebrews 4:15). He was persecuted for a righteous life, tempted in the desert and died in a most hideous way. Our Saviour understands our temptation because he too was tempted. Because Jesus loves us, he reminds us that we aren't fooling him, and we don't need to remain distant because we think he can't relate to us. At those moments, we can remember that Jesus knows, understands and cares for us because he's been there.

Prayer: *Dear God of compassion, help us to acknowledge our sins and seek your love and forgiveness. Amen*

Thought for the day: Like me, Jesus has been tempted and understands my struggle.

Michael Wolff (Colorado, US)

Send Someone Else!

Read Exodus 4:1–12

The Lord said to [Moses], 'Who gave human beings their mouths?… Is it not I, the Lord? Now go; I will help you speak and will teach you what to say.'

Exodus 4:11–12 (NIV)

Ever since I was twelve years old, attending church each week has given me a sense of peace; it lifts my spirit and helps me to face the week ahead. But sometimes I have left church thinking, 'That sermon didn't do much for me.'

Recently, one sermon started tugging at my heart more powerfully than any had before. It was about serving Christ—not just letting the church serve me. Shortly after hearing that sermon, I read in the church notices of a need for Sunday school teachers. Was this God talking to me? It couldn't be—I've never been good with children. When I told my friends that I was considering teaching, they laughed and said, 'You'll be eaten alive!'

I thought of the excuses Moses made when God asked him to lead the Israelites from slavery to the promised land. Like Moses, I wanted to say to God, 'Please send someone else!' It took a full year of resisting God's voice before I finally said, 'OK, God, I will trust you,' and began teaching children at Sunday school.

One Sunday a boy who had always seemed uninterested in participating asked to speak to me after class. He said, 'Miss, can I tell you about how I became a Christian?' I knew then that God had equipped me to serve my church.

Prayer: *Dear God, help us to hear your voice and trust you when you call us to serve you in new ways. Amen*

Thought for the day: Even with all my doubts and fears I can bring others closer to Christ.

Melissa Ramoo (New South Wales, Australia)

Power to Persevere

Read Psalm 18:1–6

I can do all things through Christ which strengtheneth me.
Philippians 4:13 (KJV)

'Christ gives us power to persevere.' These words have been written on the notice board in my family's kitchen since January 2003. At the time, I was in the habit of writing *The Upper Room*'s Thought for the Day on the noticeboard so that the whole family could meditate on it during the day. However, a family crisis occurred around the time I wrote, 'Christ gives us power to persevere', and the saying has remained on our noticeboard ever since. These words have reminded us to rely on Christ's strength again and again.

The Bible tells us that God alone is the source of our strength (Psalm 18:1; 28:7) and that we gain strength by waiting upon the Lord (Isaiah 40:31). The apostle Paul learned this lesson through his 'thorn in the flesh' (2 Corinthians 12:7). We too can learn from difficult experiences.

Our notice board reminder that God through Christ empowers us to endure has seen our family through my grandma's decade-long illness, a family friend's suicide, my dad's cancer diagnosis, and the deaths of my grandma and my dad. In the years since then, these words have been a daily comfort to my mum and me. Rather than being a thought for a single day, the promise of Christ's strength can be an encouraging reminder for us each and every day.

Prayer: *Dear God, thank you for daily reminders of your love. Help us to rely on your strength each day. Amen*

Thought for the day: Christ is my strength, today and every day.

Janine A. Kuty (Virginia, US)

Living Water

Read John 4:7–15

Jesus… cried out, 'Let anyone who is thirsty come to me, and let the one who believes in me drink. As the scripture has said, "Out of the believer's heart shall flow rivers of living water."' Now he said this about the Spirit, which believers in him were to receive.
John 7:37–39 (NRSV)

I live in Texas, which can be extremely hot and dry in the summer. We recently endured a long, severe summer drought. Lakes that had once been filled with boats were dry, cracked earth. People walked across rivers where they had previously gone swimming. Lawns that had been lush and green were dry and brown.

The following spring we finally received heavy rains. Grass that was parched and dry became thick, lush and green. Happy boaters and swimmers returned to the lakes and rivers.

At low points in my life, my soul has felt dry and parched. My spirit probably has resembled a brown lawn or a dry river bed. But by reaching out to God through prayer, worship and Bible reading, my spirit flourishes again. Once again, my soul flows with God's fresh and renewing water. God offers us a way to quench our thirst by drinking our fill of the living water he offers through Jesus Christ. The water God provides can restore what appears dry beyond recovery.

Prayer: *Dear God, when dry times come, we know that you offer living water that refills and renews our souls. Amen*

Thought for the day: God's living water quenches my thirst.

Dennis Burk (Texas, US)

God's Timing

Read Philippians 4:4–9

'Peace I leave with you; my peace I give you. I do not give to you as the world gives. Do not let your hearts be troubled and do not be afraid.'
John 14:27 (NIV)

Throughout the Gospels Jesus tells his followers not to fear. Yet when I look at the notes I've written in the margins of my Bible, I find many concerns and worries. I pray about them, and in my anxiety I want God to answer straight away. However, some of these concerns are ones I have prayed about for several years seemingly without any answers. Only later, when I look back, can I see God's hand in these situations. He heard my pleas but the answers were often different, even better, from what I expected.

During times when I doubted that my prayers were being heard, God helped me to learn patience, understanding and empathy for others. God gives us all time to grow and to become stronger. In the process we learn never to give up. Now when I am tempted to worry, I try to give my troubles to God completely and not to expect quick and easy answers.

Worry robs us of joy and peace; but Jesus says, 'Do not let your hearts be troubled' (John 14:27). If we truly trust God's loving provision in our life, we can rely on him to respond to our call—in his time. All the time our hearts can rest in that knowledge and find God's peace.

Prayer: *Heavenly Father, calm our anxious hearts. Comfort us in our distress, and help us trust you more fully. Amen*

Thought for the day: God's timing is always perfect.

Phyllis Stone Church (Kentucky, US)

PRAYER FOCUS: TO LET GO OF WORRIES AND FEARS

God of the Nomad

Read Daniel 3:8–30

The Lord, he it is that doth go before thee; he will be with thee, he will not fail thee, neither forsake thee: fear not, neither be dismayed.
Deuteronomy 31:8 (KJV)

International migration is on the rise, and its scope, complexity and impact continue to grow. Travelling to a new place can come with anxiety and fear of the unknown. The Israelites often reacted to such anxiety by turning to other gods and incurring God's wrath as they moved to new lands.

However, new environments can also offer opportunities to deepen our faith, as seen in the life of Abram when God asked him to leave his home to go to a strange land. The stories of Joseph and of Shadrach, Meshach and Abednego show how we can cultivate the presence of God, even in unfamiliar places. In the end, what really matters is that we endeavour to follow God's will wherever he leads us.

The Bible has been my companion through all my journeys, helping me to look to God, to study and to focus on his word rather than on my environment. Choosing to trust and focus on God's never-failing love and provision can strengthen us for all the changes of life.

Prayer: *Dear God, teach us to trust and obey you no matter what our circumstances may be. Amen*

Thought for the day: I can trust and obey the Lord wherever I am.

Felix Kwabena Donkor (Gauteng, South Africa)

I Just Do

Read 1 John 4:7–18

I have loved you with an everlasting love.
Jeremiah 31:3 (NIV)

I raise guinea fowl, which are fairly common on farms in the southern United States. Like chickens, these birds eat insects and have a special fondness for ticks, which makes them great additions to farms with livestock. They also create a cacophonous uproar at the arrival of guests or at anything that seems unusual to them, earning them the nickname 'watchdog'.

Unfortunately they are also rather stupid creatures. I have known them to drown themselves accidentally, to fly into fences and break their necks, and to hang upside down for long periods after getting a toe trapped in a cage. They often fly over a fence into an area where my potbellied pigs spend the day and then march back and forth for hours in front of the gate, apparently forgetting that if they can fly in then they can fly back out.

One day, as I was feeding the guinea fowl, I looked at them and thought, 'Why do I love these birds? I don't know why. I just do.' It suddenly dawned on me that God may feel something like this about us: 'Why do I love these people? I just do.' I am so grateful that God loves us, despite our forgetfulness, poor decisions and mistakes. No matter what we do, God loves us!

Prayer: *Dear Lord, thank you for loving us no matter what. Help us to love others in the same manner. Amen*

Thought for the day: How can I share God's unconditional love with others?

Rebecca Martino (Tennessee, US)

Fox Wisdom

Read Deuteronomy 31:1–8
God has said, 'Never will I leave you; never will I forsake you.'
Hebrews 13:5 (NIV)

As I drove cautiously up my long driveway, I saw a thin red fox sitting on the verge and watching over her three rambunctious babies. Not wanting to frighten them, I pulled over as the frisky trio leaped and rolled one another down the driveway, seemingly oblivious to their mother's presence. Patiently, she followed, never taking her eyes off them.

Then it occurred to me how in this moment the attentive mother fox mirrored God's care for me. She quietly allowed her babies complete freedom in unknown territory while being constantly available to guide their way. Our reading for today records that just before transferring leadership to Joshua, Moses spoke about the law and urged the people to trust God fully. God has promised never to leave or forsake us. And yet, how often have I wrestled with something all by myself, ignoring God because I was too preoccupied to see my divine parent near me, offering to help?

For me, the glimpse of that red fox reflected a very small measure of God's infinite care. I realised that, regardless of the challenges and changes that come into our lives, we can trust in God's unfailing love and presence.

Prayer: *Dear God of the ages, give us grace to live every day confident that you are trustworthy and always present with us. Amen*

Thought for the day: God's caring presence gives me freedom.

Gael Stuart Phaneuf (Colorado, US)

In the Face of Loss

Read Job 1:1–21

[Job] said, 'Naked I came from my mother's womb, and naked shall I return there; the Lord gave, and the Lord has taken away; blessed be the name of the Lord.'

Job 1:21 (NRSV)

The ultrasound technician moved the probe over my abdomen. With a concerned look on her face, she said, 'I am so sorry; there is no heart-beat. The baby has died.' My heart sank as tears rolled down my face. I nodded that I understood, even though I didn't understand at all.

This loss helped me to sympathise even more with Job, a man of great wealth with many servants, much livestock, ten children and a high standing in his community. According to today's reading, Job followed God faithfully and God considered him blameless and upright. Even so, all at once Job lost everything. In the midst of heartache, Job still had the faith to worship. At the lowest point of his life, he fell to the ground before God saying, 'Blessed be the name of the Lord.'

No one understands why tragedy occurs, but it happens to all of us. After losing my baby, I spent many months in heartache and prayer. In time, I was able to accept what had happened. At that point I could join with Job in saying, 'Blessed be the name of the Lord' and thank God for all the blessings I have received.

Prayer: *Dear Father, thank you for all your blessings. Help us to worship and acknowledge you, even when we mourn. Amen*

Thought for the day: I will praise God in both my sorrow and my joy.

Sarah Lyons (Kansas, US)

The Light of the World

Read John 12:44–50

Jesus said, 'I am the light of the world. Whoever follows me will never walk in darkness, but will have the light of life.'
John 8:12 (NIV)

Both our home and the church where my wife and I serve are located outside the city. This allows me the opportunity truly to appreciate the wonders of nature day and night. I particularly enjoy the radiance of the full moon spilling its light across the countryside.

The moon has no light source of its own but reflects the sun's light. Yet while the moon orbits Earth approximately every 27 days, its gravitational forces are at work all the time, affecting the tides among other things.

Today's reading reminds us that Jesus Christ is the light of the world, and we are to encourage others by sharing that light in our lives. Like the moon, we do not own the light but reflect the light supplied continuously by our own light source, Jesus Christ. The light of Christ is for all people, and when we reflect that light, we live in hope that all the world will 'have the light of life'.

Prayer: *Creator God, thank you for the gift of your light of love. Help us to offer it generously to others. Amen*

Thought for the day: God calls me to reflect the light of Christ to the world.

Hernaldo Lara (Carazo, Nicaragua)

Marvel at God's Love

Read Jeremiah 29:10–14

'I know the plans I have for you,' declares the Lord, 'plans to prosper you and not to harm you, plans to give you hope and a future.'
Jeremiah 29:11 (NIV)

I have been going through many challenges recently, and I trust that God will help me. But sometimes doubt creeps in, and I feel overwhelmed or helpless. After watching an episode of my favourite TV show where a team of intelligent people saved the world dressed as comic book superheroes, I wondered: 'Why can't I be a superhero? Why can't I have super powers that I can use to save millions of lives, right wrongs and bring justice to the world?' As soon as I had asked these questions the answers came to me. We are all superheroes! Our faith is our armour, our unique talents are our powers and our strength is our God!

Each day God presents us with opportunities to right wrongs by sharing Christ's love, to save lives by acting with kindness and compassion, and to bring justice by spreading his word. Our actions may not seem as big or as bold as those of the superheroes on TV. We may never know if our actions renew someone's faith or if our compassion rekindles someone's hope. We may never know whether we are an answer to someone's prayer. But as today's reading assures us, God has a plan for us. Embracing daily opportunities to help others can be a big part of that plan.

Prayer: *Dear God, help us always to trust you and your never-failing love for us. Amen*

Thought for the day: What 'super powers' has God given me to help the world?

Kathy Morgan (Maryland, US)

Christ is the Centre

Read Colossians 1:9–23

Through [his son] God was pleased to reconcile to himself all things, whether on earth or in heaven, by making peace through the blood of his cross.
Colossians 1:20 (NRSV)

Years ago, my husband and I were called to help reconcile a father and son who had undergone years of bitter feuding and separation. A round table in the centre of the room separated the two sides of the conflict during the entire discussion. It also kept them from punching each other.

When they both confessed to being servants of our Lord Jesus Christ, the mediation became centred on the element that united them: Christ. With Christ at the centre of their lives, they reached what seemed to be impossible—the reconciliation of two men and their families.

When we are reconciled with Christ, we can also be reconciled with one another because we are all members of the Body of Christ.

Prayer: *Dear God, our great mediator, thank you for reconciling us with yourself and with one another through Jesus Christ. As Jesus taught us, we pray, 'Our Father which art in heaven, Hallowed be thy name. Thy kingdom come, Thy will be done in earth, as it is in heaven. Give us this day our daily bread. And forgive us our debts, as we forgive our debtors. And lead us not into temptation, but deliver us from evil: For thine is the kingdom, and the power, and the glory, for ever.'* Amen*

Thought for the day: I can forgive because, through Christ, I am forgiven.

Charlotte Mande Ilunga (Cape Town, South Africa)

* Matthew 6:9–13 (KJV)

10,000 Reasons

Read Psalm 126:1–6

Bless the Lord, O my soul, and all that is within me, bless his holy name. Bless the Lord, O my soul, and do not forget all his benefits.
Psalm 103:1–2 (NRSV)

One morning I heard a song that mentions having 10,000 reasons to bless the Lord. As I listened, I asked myself if I have 10,000 reasons to be grateful.

I began to think about the blessing of waking up to a new day and the blessings of my children, wife, parents, siblings, in-laws and church family. I thought about the homes I have lived in, the clothes I have worn, and the other provisions I have enjoyed throughout my life. I thought about how each day is filled with at least one of these blessings. Waking up yesterday was a blessing just as waking up today is a new gift and blessing from God.

I began to count my reasons to be thankful. At 39 years of age, I have 365 days multiplied by 39 years of waking each morning—14,235 reasons to magnify God! Add to that over 16 years of marriage, and the blessing of having my two parents present for my entire life. As I considered all my days without accidents, days with my children, days with my best friend and days with grandparents, in-laws, and siblings, my heart has found well over 10,000 reasons to bless the Lord's holy name. Each day God is merciful and gracious in new ways.

Prayer: *O God, help us to see each new day as a blessing from you and live life as a way of giving thanks. Amen*

Thought for the day: What new blessing can I be thankful for today?

Cassius Rhue (South Carolina, US)

Sharing God's Word

Read Isaiah 55:8–13

The Lord said, 'My word… that goeth forth out of my mouth… shall not return unto me void, but it shall accomplish that which I please.'
Isaiah 55:11 (KJV)

My friend Robin was discouraged. Only 13 children had attended our church's annual holiday Bible club. 'We put all this money into it,' she said. 'I recruited people too. I took the week off from work, and only 13 children came.'

I told her about my first holiday Bible club. It was hosted by a small church, and only a handful of neighbourhood children attended. I was one of them. 'That's where I received my first Bible,' I told her. 'I also memorised my first Bible verse, and sang "Jesus loves me" for the first time. Thirteen years later, when a friend shared the gospel with me and quoted John 3:16, I already knew the verse, because I had memorised it so many years ago.'

I didn't make a decision to follow Christ that summer. The kind people at that church never knew I came to faith 13 years later, but God used the verse they helped me memorise to open my heart. I've served God faithfully for over 30 years. Even if we can't see it at the time, we can trust that God's word always accomplishes his purpose.

Prayer: *Dear Jesus, help us to share your word faithfully and to trust you to accomplish your purpose in those around us. Amen*

Thought for the day: Sharing God's good news is never a waste of time.

Lori Hatcher (South Carolina, US)

'Follow Me!'

Read John 21:15–23

[Jesus] said to [Peter], 'Follow me.'
John 21:19 (NRSV)

In today's reading we find Jesus talking to Peter after Peter has denied him. Jesus tries to help him to focus on his own life. However, Peter instantly asks about another disciple and what might happen to him.

I have acted like Peter at times. I look at others' lives and begin comparing my life to theirs. Why has God allowed them such good fortune and not me? Why don't I have a husband, children, a nice house or a certain job? But when I start comparing, I become frustrated and dissatisfied with my life.

Jesus' answer to me is the same as it was to Peter: 'What is that to you? You must follow me.' Jesus knows I can become distracted by looking at others' lives. All he wants from me is to focus on what he has called me to do.

We all have unique abilities and talents that God can use. No two of us are completely the same. Even if God does not give us something we want, we can trust that his plans for us are always good. When we accept the life God has given us and live it well, we can be content.

Prayer: *Dear heavenly Father, thank you for loving us. We are yours. Help us to live life in ways that glorify you. Amen*

Thought for the day: God always wants the best for me.

Melissa Wilson (Kansas, US)

The Old Watch

Read Joshua 24:14–17

Cast all your anxiety on [God], because he cares for you.
1 Peter 5:7 (NRSV)

As a minister, I recently received an appointment to a new congregation. I was packing and waiting for the big change in my life when I saw my grandmother's old watch, which she had received from her father. It was more than 60 years old and still working.

The evening before leaving my home for the last time, I thought about my life and recalled the life of my grandmother. The old watch had counted out her hours in this world and the hours of her father's life, and I know it was counting out the hours of my life as well, a life I enjoy as a gift from God. And I thought, 'What will my service be like? What example will I leave behind?' I remembered the words of Psalm 90:12: 'So teach us to count our days that we may gain a wise heart.'

We do not have much time in this world; we do not know when the hands of our life's watch will stop. But what we do know is that our loving God has given us life and the ability to choose how we will live it. May our lives be full of faith, hope and love for all that God has created!

Prayer: *Dear Lord, lead us on your way and give us wise hearts so we can remain faithful to you, our loving Creator. Amen*

Thought for the day: How am I showing gratitude for the life God has given me?

Vladimir Angelov (Ruse, Bulgaria)

The Great Exchange

Read 1 Samuel 1:1–18

Do not worry about anything, but in everything by prayer and supplication with thanksgiving let your requests be made known to God. And the peace of God, which surpasses all understanding, will guard your hearts and your minds in Christ Jesus.
Philippians 4:6–7 (NRSV)

We were miles from the nearest town. With the low-petrol warning light illuminated in my vehicle and two mountains to cross, I prayed, 'Our mobile phones don't work out here, and we're two young women who don't want to walk these roads in the dark. Please help us arrive safely.' After I had prayed, I continued to worry until we reached our destination safely.

Later, when I read about Hannah's prayer, I thought about our trip and my prayer. Her prayer showed me that I had missed out on one of the benefits of praying. Hannah had made her request to God, and 'then… went on her way, ate some food, and wasn't sad any longer' (1 Samuel 1:18, CEB). Hannah released her anxiety to God and found peace even before he answered her. In contrast, I didn't fully release my worry until after God had answered my prayer and we had arrived safely at the next town. Rather than thanking God for hearing my prayer and trusting that an answer would come, I continued to worry until I'd seen the outcome.

Hannah's story taught me that one of the great gifts of prayer is to know that God will answer, even if we don't know when or how. When we pray, we can immediately thank him for the answer that will come. Doing so can allow us to let go of our concerns and begin to accept the peace God offers us.

Prayer: *Dear God, thank you for answering our prayers and for your peace that guards our minds and hearts. Amen*

Bethany Hayes (Oregon, US)

Perfect Love

Read Romans 8:31–39

Love has been perfected among us in this: that we may have boldness on the day of judgement, because as he is, so are we in this world. There is no fear in love, but perfect love casts out fear.
1 John 4:17–18 (NRSV)

When I was a child my family did not attend church regularly. My main contact with preaching was through radio sermons that were mostly about fearing God's condemnation. I started to attend church at the age of twelve, and I was relieved to discover that the preaching there was much different. The focus was on God's love for us and our love for others. But a part of me worried that our church might be watering down the Bible's message.

Then one day I came across today's quoted verse. I was overjoyed to discover that God does not want us to live in fear of condemnation. Such fearful love is incomplete, immature and imperfect. The loving message I heard at church is true.

I am now a minister, and I encourage my church members not to fear the condemnation of God or of other people who claim we are not true Christians because our beliefs and practices differ from theirs. Paul's message to the Romans in today's reading reminds us, 'It is God who justifies. Who is to condemn?' (Romans 8:33–34). As followers of Christ, we can know that nothing can separate us from the love of God (see Romans 8:38–39). Thanks be to God!

Prayer: *Gracious God, free us from fear, and help us to embrace the truth that through the death and resurrection of Jesus Christ we are justified by your grace. Amen*

Thought for the day: Nothing can separate us from God's love.

Michael A. Macdonald (North Carolina, US)

Discernment

Read 2 Timothy 3:14–17

All scripture is inspired by God and is useful for teaching, for reproof, for correction, and for training in righteousness, so that everyone who belongs to God may be proficient, equipped for every good work.
2 Timothy 3:16–17 (NRSV)

I found an intriguing and challenging shawl pattern. The variegated yarn had the brilliant warm hues of a sunset. As I skimmed through the directions, I thought, 'What? This makes no sense! Impossible!' I knew how to make the required stitches, but I could not visualise how the shawl could possibly result from the instructions on the printed page. Perhaps this was beyond my ability. I wondered whether I should commit to the expensive, challenging project.

Christian discernment can be like my crochet project. Feeling the urge to do something new for God, we find an intriguing service opportunity, but it appears impossible. Perhaps we know how to perform the necessary tasks, but we cannot visualise how to begin. Perhaps a particular opportunity seems beyond our abilities. We wonder whether we should commit our time and energy to it.

In the end, I trusted the crochet pattern's directions. I bought the materials, read the directions one line at a time and followed the pattern carefully. My shawl is everything I hoped it would be. In the same way, if we commit to reading the Bible a little at a time, every day, and living as it instructs, the experience will be all we hope for and more.

Prayer: *Dear God, help us to discern the next steps to take, and give us the courage to move forward. In the name of Christ, we pray. Amen*

Thought for the day: The Bible offers me tools for discernment.

Sharon B. Capron (Oklahoma, US)

Making Room

Read Proverbs 3:1–8

Forget the former things; do not dwell on the past. See, I am doing a new thing! Now it springs up; do you not perceive it? I am making a way in the wilderness and streams in the wasteland.
Isaiah 43:18–19 (NIV)

At the age of 42, I developed an ailment that affected my ability to move. My gait became uneven, my head tilted to the right and an array of other muscular problems left me weak and sore. For four years, I feared the future and prayed for strength and healing. I found hope in Isaiah 43:18–19, trusting that God was working on my behalf.

After years of living in fear, I made peace with my situation, knowing that God would be with me even if I became confined to a wheelchair or worse. I was directed to a skilled neurologist, who diagnosed me with a rare genetic condition that left my body without enough dopamine, a chemical required for proper nerve-brain function. Trusting God with my future, I began taking medicine and immediately began to improve. Within a year, I could walk, stand and move correctly.

I now rely on three doses of medicine each day, but I praise God for my body. Without my weakness I would never have known the depth of God's strength, wisdom and unconditional love. Only after I stopped trying to solve the problem myself did I make room for God to answer my prayers.

Prayer: *Dear Lord, help me to lean less on my own understanding and to turn my burdens over to you. Amen*

Thought for the day: How am I making room for God to help me?

Tamar Piehler (Georgia, US)

Promises Made and Kept

Read Hebrews 6:10–20

We have this hope as an anchor for the soul, firm and secure.
Hebrews 6:19 (NIV)

A friend once gave me an outdoor house ornament made of faceted glass balls that rotate in the wind. I hung it outside. When I awoke to sunshine the following morning, I was delighted to discover that the walls of my house were splashed with little flashing rainbows. They reminded me of God's promise to Noah never again to destroy the earth by flood.

Now, whenever I'm going through difficult times, I remember the many promises that God has made and kept: he promised Abraham that his descendants would be as numerous as the stars, and they are; he promised that Moses would lead the Israelites out of Egypt, and Moses did; God promised the people of Israel that they would return from exile, and they did. Each promise required a faithful response.

Jesus said, 'Seek first [God's] kingdom and his righteousness, and all these things will be given to you' (Matthew 6:33). In my 35-year walk with God, I have acted on this and found it to be true.

The Bible says that those who belong to God through Jesus Christ will be with him in heaven for ever. I stake my life on the truth of this promise as well. And, based on God's faithfulness, I trust that I will not be disappointed.

Prayer: *Dear God, thank you for being faithful in caring for us—no matter what. Amen*

Thought for the day: When I see a rainbow, I will remember all the promises God has made, and kept.

James Forayter (Queensland, Australia)

Keep Going

Read 2 Corinthians 12:1–10

Let us run with perseverance the race marked out for us, fixing our eyes on Jesus, the pioneer and perfecter of faith.
Hebrews 12:1–2 (NIV)

At the age of 16, when I joined a six-week bicycle trip through Holland, England and France, I found Holland manageable, but England's hills were overwhelming. I hadn't trained properly for cycling 30-50 miles daily. I was often alone and lagging behind, especially on the steep climbs. When my travel companions stopped for a quick break, they'd watch for my approach and yell, 'Keep going, Jane! Don't stop!'

Now, when I'm faced with a setback or overwhelmed by challenges, I picture God in the role of my long-ago travelling companions. But God is more than a cheerleader. He is my strength and provider. When I pray for his help to keep me going, what seems staggering at the moment becomes straightforward and possible.

Reading about the faith of others in Hebrews 11 and recalling God's words to Paul in today's reading encourages me: 'My grace is sufficient for you, for my power is made perfect in weakness.' Each trial we face is an opportunity for diligence and dedication. We can look beyond the all-consuming task toward Jesus to find the strength and encouragement to continue.

Prayer: *Dear God, thank you for opportunities to practise perseverance. Help us to become more steadfast so that we might mature in our faith. Amen*

Thought for the day: I'm able to go the distance with God as my strength.

Jane Compton (Oregon, US)

Sharing Our Plates

Read 2 Timothy 1:1–7

I am reminded of your sincere faith, a faith that lived first in your grandmother Lois and your mother Eunice and now, I am sure, lives in you.

2 Timothy 1:5 (NRSV)

When my son began eating solid foods, it was a challenge to get him to eat vegetables. Soft, bite-sized pieces of carrot, broccoli, and squash landed on the floor faster than I could spoon them onto his plate. One day I realised that although my son was uninterested in the food on his plate, he was interested in what was on mine. He would eat anything served on my plate in order to imitate me. I learned to pile my plate high with enough colourful vegetables to share with my son. Over time he developed such an appetite for vegetables that he began to enjoy them served on his own plate.

When I consider the influence of Lois and Eunice, it is evident that a similar sharing occurred in the life of Timothy. This grandmother and mother shared a spiritual plate chock-full of their faith in Christ. Over time the faith they planted grew in Timothy to become a life of faith and service to the Lord.

Parents and grandparents want to provide their children and grand-children with the very best home, education and opportunities. Lois and Eunice are reminders of our responsibility also to provide the next generation with a foundation of faith, that they may be nourished until they crave a sincere faith of their own.

Prayer: *Dear Lord, help us to live in ways that show our love for you and a sincere faith in Jesus Christ with the generations that follow us. Amen*

Thought for the day: How can I plant seeds of faith for the next generation?

Donyale Fraylon (Texas, US)

In God's Care

Read Psalm 32:8–11

I will instruct you and teach you in the way you should go; I will counsel you with my loving eye on you.
Psalm 32:8 (NIV)

I received a degree in education in 2014. After graduation, I packed my bags and travelled to another area of the country in search of a job. My plan was to work wherever I settled. I never once thought about the plans God had for my life. I left behind my family and the work I did in my church. Once I had moved, I stayed with a relative and began the job search.

Two months went by, and I was offered no job. During this time, I felt a strong longing for my family and church. I consoled myself by reading *El Aposento Alto* (*The Upper Room* Spanish edition), but I felt a great emptiness in my heart. I began to wonder if God had abandoned me, but I tried to trust that he was watching over me and caring for my well-being.

At this low point in my life, I received a call with a job offer in the place I had left. I understood this call as God's answer to my prayers. Without thinking twice about it, I packed my bags and returned. From this experience, I learned that the plans God has for me are not always the same as mine. God has always watched over me. When we continue to pray and have faith, we can be assured that he always watches over us and guides us.

Prayer: *Loving God, help us understand that you want only the best for us and that your plans are far greater than ours. Amen*

Thought for the day: God has great plans for me.

Abigail Pijal (Ecuador)

No Limits

Read Mark 9:38–41

Whoever is not against us is for us.
Mark 9:40 (NIV)

A fellow musician and I had just started a contemporary worship service with only two instruments: drums and an acoustic guitar. We did the best we could, but the worshippers struggled to sing with such limited instrumentation. In the days that followed, a teenaged member of our church kept insisting that I ask her brother to play with us. He was an incredibly talented electric guitarist, but he told me that he did not believe in God. I refused to allow an atheist to play in the church worship band. But my belief in God wasn't big enough.

Fortunately his sister was persistent, and I finally agreed to let him play. While playing with the praise team, the young man came to faith in Christ. What an important lesson I learned—that there are no limits to how God can work!

The disciples learned a similar lesson. One day John saw a man who was not part of their group casting out demons in Jesus' name. John tried to stop to it. He assumed, as I did, that God works only through our approved methods. The man didn't have proper approval! But Jesus responded, 'Do not stop him… whoever is not against us is for us' (Mark 9:39–40).

I pray that our eyes will be opened to see what God is doing in our world, especially through unlikely people in unexpected places.

Prayer: *Dear God, help us to see where you are at work and then to participate wholeheartedly. Amen*

Thought for the day: God's work in our world has no limits.

Kevin L. Thomas (Alabama, US)

The Hidden Disciple

Read Acts 12:1–5

[Jesus] saw James and John, Zebedee's sons, in their boat repairing the fishing nets. At that very moment he called them. They followed him, leaving their father, Zebedee, in the boat with the hired workers.
Mark 1:19–20 (CEB)

Jesus called James and John, who were brothers, at the same time. They followed immediately and were with Jesus throughout his ministry. Interestingly, almost every reference to James is in relation to John and Peter. He is what I call a 'hidden disciple'. After Jesus' resurrection, James went on to help build the church. He seemed to be one of Jesus' three closest friends, who sometimes were invited to experience events that the rest of the Twelve were not.

However, we know almost nothing about James' personality or ministry. He died early in the book of Acts and, unlike Stephen, whose martyrdom is described over two chapters (Acts 6—7), James' death is given one line (Acts 12:2). This does not mean that James was unimportant. Jesus called him for a purpose that played out uniquely in his life and death. We can honour James simply because we know he was a follower of Jesus.

Many followers of Christ are 'hidden' among us. Some serve in the background; others are isolated by various circumstances from the body of Christ. But Jesus cherishes every believer: he calls each of us to a unique path of discipleship and values each member of the church.

Prayer: *Thank you, Lord, that our worth to you is not measured by how well known we are to other people, for we know that none of us is hidden from your loving eyes. Amen*

Thought for the day: Christ sees and cherishes every person who follows him.

Claire Bell (South Australia, Australia)

Never an Annoyance

Read Psalm 91:1–16
May your unfailing love be my comfort.
Psalm 119:76 (NIV)

My two cats, Samantha and Chloe, both love to lie in my lap. Chloe is quite personable and affectionate. Samantha, on the other hand, seems to need constant reassurance that she is loved. Some days it seems that every time I sit down, Samantha is there waiting to jump onto my lap. At times I find her constant attention-seeking annoying.

One morning as I pushed Samantha away, I thought about how God never pushes me away when I come to him. Sometimes I feel confident in my relationship with God, and I delight in praising him as much as I do in seeking his help. At other times, I come to God in desperation, needing a place of refuge and restoration. I also need reassurance that he loves me. Many passages in the Bible tell us that God loves us and will always be with us. I never have to wonder whether God will have time for me or how I will be received. He always has time and always reaches out with loving arms.

Prayer: *Dear God, thank you for loving us and always being available to comfort and encourage us. Amen*

Thought for the day: Today I will encourage someone by showing them God's love.

Pat Luffman Rowland (Tennessee, US)

Humble Service

Read John 1:14–17

Who is wise and understanding among you? Let them show it by their good life, by deeds done in the humility that comes from wisdom.
James 3:13 (NIV)

A few days a week I volunteer at our church, helping with the various meetings that take place. I often see a certain man with a screwdriver or a drill or a sander in his hand.

When I ask him what he is doing he says, 'Oh, I noticed that there are some jobs that need to be done, and I thought I'd just come in and do them in my spare time.' He doesn't receive any pay for these important little jobs, and most of the congregation has no idea that he works there so often during the week. But it is disciples like this man who keep every church repaired and usable.

Some think that to be a disciple means witnessing to hundreds or preaching to crowds, and many disciples do these things. But no less important is the disciple who cheerfully does the little things every day that make other people's lives more pleasant and productive. We all have some kind of talent that we can devote to further our Lord's kingdom. All we have to do is identify that skill or talent, decide to use it for the Lord—and then get up and actually do it.

Prayer: *Dear Lord, help us to appreciate small acts of service done in your name by people who often go unrecognised. Amen*

Thought for the day: Whose acts of Christian service can I recognise today?

Ken Claar (Idaho, US)

The Power of Praise

Read Psalm 150:1–6

My mouth is filled with your praise, declaring your splendour all day long.
Psalm 71:8 (NIV)

Recently, the leader of my Christian youth group asked each of us why we enjoyed attending. One of my friends said with a smile, 'Because the food is always delicious.' Others replied, 'The sermon always fits our situation.' Some said they liked the conversations with each other. I said that I liked the time to praise and worship God. I like singing, and as I lift up my praises to God, I feel my heart fill with peace and joy.

My situation was not always good. I was often stressed and depressed, struggling to find words to pray. During those times, praise and worship helped me to realise that God is always with me and will never leave me alone. I felt God comforting me and whispering, 'Never will I leave you; never will I forsake you' (Hebrews 13:5). Through praise and worship, we can all connect with God who sustains and strengthens us.

Prayer: *Beloved God, thank you for being with us in all circumstances. We praise you with all our heart, soul, and strength. May our worship be pleasing to you as we pray, 'Our Father which art in heaven, Hallowed be thy name. Thy kingdom come. Thy will be done, as in heaven, so in earth. Give us day by day our daily bread. And forgive us our sins; for we also forgive every one that is indebted to us. And lead us not into temptation; but deliver us from evil.'* Amen*

Thought for the day: How will I praise and worship God today?

Meliana Santoso (East Java, Indonesia)

          * Luke 11:2–4 (KJV)

Go For the Gold

Read 1 Peter 4:8–11

Jesus said, '[The Spirit of truth] will glorify me, because he will take what is mine and declare it to you.'
John 16:14 (NRSV)

When I was 21, my best friend, Tim, and I got summer jobs in Skagway, Alaska. We'd been dating for several months, so I was delighted when he proposed and slipped a gold-nugget ring on my finger. A few months later, we married.

As prospectors carefully sift out the grit so that they can extract gold nuggets, we had a lot of filtering to do. Soon after Tim and I married, we argued about many things. For one, Tim draws his energy from being alone while I am outgoing and crave time with friends. The differences between us made me frustrated and angry.

As I came to know God better, I began to appreciate how he values me and my talents. I decided to value Tim in the same way. I complimented him on his abilities, such as writing computer software and being a good listener for our three children.

Each day, my prayers and my growing relationship with God drew Tim and me closer as well. When we choose to find goodness in our loved ones, negativity falls away. In the process, we can extend God's accepting nature to those we love.

Prayer: *Dear Holy Spirit, help us to sift through our frustration and negativity so that we can see the gold in one another. Amen*

Thought for the day: Where do I see God's gold in my loved ones?

Lynn Hare (Oregon, US)

Comforting Presence

Read Psalm 23:1–6
The Lord is my shepherd, I shall not want.
Psalm 23:1 (NRSV)

I received an unexpected phone call telling me that my dad had passed away after suffering with Alzheimer's for several years. As I travelled almost 1200 miles to be with my family, I had time to reflect on my dad's life and what a great family man and provider he had been. It was now time for me to provide strength for my family.

Over the past three decades I have struggled with alcohol and drug addiction. After surrendering to God, I have managed to remain clean and sober for some time. I was now about to participate in the celebration of my dad's life and I was thankful that God had helped me become well enough to handle this situation. Once the week had ended, I felt so grateful to have honoured my dad in a way that would have made him proud. God made me available to comfort people and made others available to comfort me. I was able to draw upon the strength of God to get through the tough moments.

As the celebration of Dad's life ended, I knew God's comforting presence. I felt joy in knowing that he walks with us through the valley and brings us safely to the other side. I now feel closer to my dad than ever before. Thanks be to God!

Prayer: *Dear God, thank you for healing the sick and giving strength to the weak. Help us to recognise every opportunity to share your love with others. Amen*

Thought for the day: God walks with me through every dark valley.

Todd Ricketts (Florida, US)

The Fig Tree

Read James 5:7–8

The end of a matter is better than its beginning, and patience is better than pride.
Ecclesiastes 7:8 (NIV)

Over two years ago, I bought a small fig tree and planted it in the garden. It didn't do well and looked as if it was dying. I dug it up and put it in a large pot. It stood in the pot for a long time, struggling to thrive. During the winter, I dug another hole in the garden where the drainage was better, and I replanted the bare tree.

With the coming of spring, I watered and inspected my tree daily. I found no sign of life. New leaves were appearing on other trees, but the fig tree was bare. It looked like a dead stick. I gave up all hope of its reviving. Yet some time later, I saw the tiniest tip of a green bud. The fig tree eventually came to life, and recently we ate our first fig from it.

As I write this, I see that nothing and no one is too far gone for God. Just as I persisted in resettling my tree as it struggled to grow, so God is continually resettling, redirecting and moving us along into growth and fruitful production. The process can be uncomfortable and challenging, but we are assured, as we place ourselves in God's hands, that new life and fruit will spring forth in time.

Prayer: *Dear Lord, help me to be patient as you work in and with me to bring about new life. Amen*

Thought for the day: God only requires me to take one step at a time.

Joan Lake (New South Wales, Australia)

Working for the Lord

Read Ephesians 6:5–9

Render service with enthusiasm, as to the Lord and not to men and women.

Ephesians 6:7 (NRSV)

In my late twenties, a few years after I had committed my life to Christ, I was working as a computer programmer for a large company. One day I had been so unsuccessful in searching for an error in a computer program I had written that I began to question my vocational choice. I remember praying, 'Lord, I would prefer to serve you full time.' I had always thought that God called only ministers, church workers and missionaries to full-time Christian service. But that day, I sensed God telling me, 'You already serve me full time. I have placed you with this company.'

I learned from this experience that God delights in our honest work in various occupations. He calls some people to serve as ministers and church workers and he also calls Christians to serve in their homes and in many different workplaces.

In whatever we do, we can work at it enthusiastically as if for the Lord and not for people (see Colossians 3:23). We are called to serve with integrity and a positive attitude so that, whatever our occupation, we will bring glory to God.

Prayer: *Dear God, help us to work in ways that bring you honour and praise. Amen*

Thought for the day: I will serve the Lord where I am today.

Whitney V. Myers (Pennsylvania, US)

Server Available 24/7

Read Psalm 34:1–18

This poor man called, and the Lord heard him; he saved him out of all his troubles.
Psalm 34:6 (NIV)

When we were given computers to improve learning opportunities for our high school students, we were keen to thank the donors and well-wishers who had helped us. We wanted to contact them as soon as we were connected to the internet.

When we had composed our messages and were ready to send our emails, the server was not available. It took several minutes to connect, but the moment the server was available the speed of communication was beyond our expectations.

Computers have provided us with a technology that allows us to reach people far and near in no time—if the server that provides quick service is available. But for all who have faith in Jesus the lines to Almighty God are open at any time in any conditions. We need only to call on God with a sincere heart. He is ready to listen to our prayers, because we have sought a genuine connection through our Lord Jesus Christ.

Prayer: *Dear God, thank you for your promise to hear us. Help us to trust that you are always listening. In Jesus' name. Amen*

Thought for the day: God is always available to hear our prayers.

Benjamin R. K. Lall (Assam, India)

PRAYER FOCUS: SOMEONE STRUGGLING WITH TECHNOLOGY

A Way to Remember

Read Joshua 4:18–24

[Joshua] said to the Israelites, 'In the future when your descendants ask their parents, "What do these stones mean?" tell them, "Israel crossed the Jordan on dry ground." '
Joshua 4:21–22 (NIV)

When I had finished reading aloud a meditation to a friend, she reached into her coat pocket. Her hand revealed a small, smooth, pink stone. She told me that she always puts it into her pocket as a reminder to pause for reflection during the day—to give thanks to God for all the blessings she has received, to look past her mundane tasks and see afresh the beauty in a moment, to quiet her heart and catch a glimpse of God nearby. Whenever my friend grasps her small stone, it prompts her to stop and remember.

In today's reading, the Israelites gathered twelve stones for the same purpose—to remember. These twelve stones were significant because the Israelites collected them from the dry riverbed as they crossed the Jordan. Each stone represented a tribe of Israel, symbolising the Israelites' deliverance from Egypt. Whenever the Israelites looked at the stones, they would remember how God had intervened in a mighty way.

God also encourages us to remember. When we consider his goodness and love in the past, we find courage to trust him for the days ahead.

Prayer: *Dear God, help us to think of you throughout each day. May we catch glimpses of you and remember your goodness to us. Amen*

Thought for the day: Remembering God's faithfulness in the past gives me hope for the future.

Lin Daniels (Massachusetts, US)

Spirit of Joy

Read Psalm 98:1–9

Shout for joy to the Lord, all the earth. Worship the Lord with gladness; come before him with joyful songs… give thanks to him and praise his name.
Psalm 100:1–2, 4 (NIV)

The 88-year-old woman had come to the soup kitchen for her supper. She seemed to be the life of the party at her table, encouraging everyone around her. Apparently hard of hearing, she talked loudly, which allowed many people to hear the 'Bless you!' that she said to those who stopped to greet her.

Prior to the meal, many of the people who entered the dining area looked downcast and seemed ashamed to be there. However, the Spirit of God, working through this positive and joyful lady, seemed to change the atmosphere of the whole room. In no time, the laughter and relaxed fellowship at her table had spread to all the other tables.

Serving the Lord with gladness is contagious and brings joy to the heart. It helps us to understand that no matter what our circumstances are, we can be agents of God's blessings.

Prayer: *Helper of all people, please help us to be positive and joyful witnesses for you wherever we are. Amen*

Thought for the day: God can help me bring joy to others through my joyful attitude.

Walter N. Maris (Missouri, US)

PRAYER FOCUS: SOMEONE WHO IS HOMELESS

By Still Waters

Read John 10:14–18

Jesus said, 'I am the good shepherd. I know my own and my own know me.'

John 10:14 (NRSV)

Once when I was out walking after a heavy thunderstorm, I saw some sheep desperate to get away from flood waters and onto higher ground. But they were obstructed by deep water in front of the gate. Scared and bleating loudly, they started to panic, running around in circles.

Soon I saw the shepherd rushing toward the sheep. She shouted and they stopped running, reassured by her familiar voice.

She put planks over the water and walked across to the group of sheep. She spoke to them softly all the time, and they became quiet and calm. It seemed that they knew from experience that they could trust their shepherd. She urged the nearest ewe to walk with her across the wooden path to the safety of higher ground. The other sheep watched, and they too began to follow. Soon they had all followed the shepherd and were safely away from the dangerous waters.

This experience reminded me of the way Jesus, our Good Shepherd, comes running when we call and walks with us through stormy waters. Jesus Christ will always lead us on the right path.

Prayer: *Dear God, hear us when we cry out, and help us to trust that you will lead us to where we should be. Amen*

Thought for the day: Christ hears my cry and will lead me to safety.

Pam Lewis (Essex, England)

A Prayer for Peace

Read John 14:23–27

Turn from evil and do good; seek peace and pursue it.
Psalm 34:14 (NIV)

Frustrating days and sleepless nights prompted me to share my troubling situation with my friend Jerry when we met for our weekly prayer time. I asked Jerry for advice. He cautiously offered me some suggestions, but they brought no clear solution to my dilemma. Later, though, when Jerry prayed, 'Lord, give Steve peace', the answer surfaced. Jerry's prayer melted the tension because peace was what I had been missing. God's peace doesn't come as a result of problems solved; it is present amidst the problems.

Later, Jerry's prayer reminded me of an incident from my youth. One day during a fierce blizzard I walked into a small grove of trees. Because the trees diffused the fury of the storm, the wooded area was calm and peaceful; birds fluttered from branch to branch and wildlife scampered in the soft, powdery snow. The snowflakes dropped gently from the sky because there was no wind. Still, as I looked beyond the trees, the fierce storm raged.

Jerry's prayer continues to bring me relief as I remember that God's peace, like a grove of trees, can shelter me from the storms of life.

Prayer: *Dear Father God, give us your peace which is beyond our understanding so that we can face today's struggles with courage. Amen*

Thought for the day: How will I seek God's peace today?

Steven Thompson (Iowa, US)

Let the Children Come

Read Luke 18:15–17

From the lips of children and infants you, Lord, have called forth your praise.
Matthew 21:16 (NIV)

I was eight years old when a preacher came to our church to run an evangelistic mission. I heard him preach and he finished with a prayer during which he asked anyone who wanted to give their life to Jesus to raise their hand. I didn't even peep through my hands to see if anyone did, but when I got home I burst into tears. 'What's the matter?' asked my parents. 'I didn't put my hand up,' I cried, 'and I should have done.' Fortunately I had understanding parents who helped me with a prayer there and then as I dedicated my young life to Christ.

I have a card in my Bible that says 'My Decision' and I've had it now for nearly 60 years! The card includes the words: 'I know whom I have believed, and am convinced that he is able to guard what I have entrusted to him' (2 Timothy 1:12). I wrote my name and address and the date—September 1957—on the card and can declare that God is faithful to his word.

I remain grateful for my parents' guidance and for those others in my church who welcomed me to a relationship with Christ when I was young. Children can be noisy in church, they can fidget and talk and appear not to take part in the service. But let us never show disapproval or feel that they are unworthy of Jesus' love and care. He made it quite clear that he welcomes children into his kingdom, and so should we.

Prayer: *Thank you, Lord Jesus, that your love has no boundaries. May we help children into an understanding of you as Lord and Saviour. Amen*

Thought for the day: Nobody is too young to come to Jesus.

Pam Pointer (Wiltshire, England)

A Good Representative

Read 2 Corinthians 5:16–21

We are ambassadors for Christ, since God is making his appeal through us; we entreat you on behalf of Christ, be reconciled to God.
2 Corinthians 5:20 (NRSV)

Years ago, six of my relatives and I accompanied another relative to her in-laws' home after her wedding. As is our custom, our contingent included people representing the parents of the bride. Anesu, in his early twenties, represented the father. He took his role seriously and represented the family well. He even refrained from showing off his wild dance moves during the party after the wedding. To my surprise, the in-laws treated Anesu with the respect and honour usually reserved for older people in our culture.

When we had fulfilled our responsibility, one elder commented that Anesu was a good representative.

This made me wonder what makes a good representative. From this experience, I learned that a representative has authority from the one they represent, carries the interests of the one they represent and knows well the one they represent. These same qualities make us good ambassadors for Christ. We derive our authority from Jesus Christ; we represent Christ's interests and concerns as described in scripture, and we know Christ through prayer and worship. I am a good representative when I cease to live for myself and live for Christ.

Prayer: *Dear God, help us to know you more fully so that we can be true and faithful representatives of you wherever we go. Amen*

Thought for the day: How can I represent God well today?

Maaraidzo E. Mutambara (Manicaland, Zimbabwe)

Beyond Understanding

Read 1 John 5:1–14

This is the confidence we have in approaching God: that if we ask anything according to his will, he hears us.
1 John 5:14 (NIV)

For years my daughter has suffered from frequent, severe migraine headaches that only medication and a dark, quiet room can lessen. Seeing this, I feel helpless and wish I could suffer in her place; but I can't. So for three years now I have been praying for her healing—fervently, hopefully, confidently, and with as much faith as I can muster. And yet my daughter continues to experience this pain that I can't make better.

The Bible tells us that we will receive if we ask. But it also tells of two sets of disciples who prayed for two different men of God to be released from prison. I'm sure both groups prayed fervently, hopefully, confidently, and with as much faith as they could muster. Yet an angel freed Peter, and John the Baptist was executed. Did Peter's disciples pray harder than John's disciples? If not, why does God seem to answer some prayers and not others?

Surely God hears all our prayers and answers us. Sometimes the answer is immediate; sometimes he says, 'Not now.' And sometimes we may never know the answer. I will continue to pray for my daughter, knowing that God's love for her is even greater than mine. I trust that God hears us and responds in ways beyond our understanding.

Prayer: *Dear God, help us to trust that you will always respond to our prayers, though we may never understand the timing or the answer. Amen*

Thought for the day: God sees a big picture that is beyond my range of vision.

Tom Smith (Utah, US)

Small Group Questions

Wednesday 3 May

1. Do you think it should be easier for a person to 'control their demons' if they are a Christian? Why or why not?

2. What scripture passages come to mind when you think about God's grace and forgiveness? Which of these are most encouraging for you?

3. Have you ever found it difficult to forgive yourself for something you have done? Why was it difficult? Is it helpful to know that God forgives us and forgets about what we have done? Why or why not?

4. Think of a situation in your life today in which you would like to have a fresh start. What is the situation and what would it look like for you to start afresh?

5. How does your church talk about and demonstrate forgiveness? Give an example of a time when someone in your church needed or showed forgiveness. What did you learn from this example?

Wednesday 10 May

1. The writer of today's meditation says, 'God is both mother and father for us.' Do you agree with her? Why or why not?

2. Can you think of other scripture passages where God is depicted more like a mother than a father? Which of these passages speak to you most? What other descriptions of God in scripture are meaningful to you?

3. What images or characteristics come to mind when you think of your earthly mother? Which of these attributes does God have? Did you come to know God in this way from personal experience or from scripture?

4. Do you read and study one translation of the Bible or several translations? What are some of the possible benefits of reading and studying more than one translation?

5. Are you part of a small-group Bible study? If so, what topics does your group discuss? What has been the most memorable topic for you? Why is it the most memorable?

Wednesday 17 May

1. Think of an experience similar to the writer of today's meditation in which someone has shown you kindness. How did it feel to be treated with such compassion? In what ways was your experience similar to that of the writer?

2. What does scripture say about how we are to treat other people? Is there one scripture passage that is most meaningful to you? Why is it most meaningful to you? Name a few ways you try to put this passage into practice.

3. When in your daily life have you witnessed an exemplary act of compassion? What did you learn from this experience? Did it change your understanding of compassion in any way? If so, how?

4. When has showing compassion to someone been particularly challenging for you? Why? What did you do?

5. In what ways does your church encourage acts of compassion toward others? Name some specific acts of compassion you can show to someone in your community of faith today.

Wednesday 24 May

1. Have you ever felt hurt because someone did not include you in their plans? What other feelings did you experience toward this person? How did this affect your relationship?

2. When has a child taught you an important life lesson? What did they teach you? How might your church learn from the children in your congregation?

3. Is it easy or difficult for you to forgive someone who has hurt you? When did you last forgive someone for hurting you?

4. Have you ever hurt someone and needed forgiveness from them? Did you ask that person for forgiveness? What was this experience like for you? What did you learn from it?

5. Think of examples in scripture where Jesus forgave those who were hurting him. What do these examples teach us about forgiveness?

Wednesday 31 May

1. Do you agree with the writer of today's meditation when he says that we should go to church with the attitude of what we can put into it? Why or why not?

2. Do you think worship is important? Why or why not? Do you go to worship every Sunday? What do you like most about your church service? What do you like least?

3. If you could change one aspect of your church service, what would it be and why would you change it?

4. Have you ever been guilty of making the same complaint overheard by the writer? In what ways might today's meditation change what you say or do the next time you are tempted to complain about a church service?

5. The writer says that we can meet the needs of people within our congregations by complimenting them, volunteering, contributing financially and praying for them. In what other ways can we, as people of faith, meet others' needs?

Wednesday 7 June

1. Has there ever been a time in your journey of faith when you have given all of something you have in order to help another person? Who was the person and what did you give?

2. Can you think of other occasions in scripture when someone gave all of what they had to God? Which of these stories do you find most encouraging? Most discouraging? Why?

3. When has someone given you all of something very costly or important to them? How did this make you feel? After the experience, did it influence how you give to others?

4. At the end of today's meditation the writer asks, 'Will we give God only a little here and a little there, or will we break ourselves open and pour ourselves out to him?' How would you respond to this question?

5. How does your church pour itself out for the surrounding community? What ministries, offerings or relationships does your church support? How might you participate and pour yourself out by doing God's work today?

Wednesday 14 June

1. How do you think God sees you? Is there anything about this picture that you would like to change? If so, what? How would you like other people to see you?

2. How do you picture God? Why do you think of him as having these particular attributes? How did you come to think of him in this way? Has your image of God changed over time?

3. Has there ever been a person in your life whom you disliked because they reminded you of something you disliked in yourself? What could this experience teach you not only about other people but about yourself?

4. When have you had a difficult time loving something about yourself? Why was it difficult? What did you do? Did you try to change yourself or change the way you felt about that characteristic?

5. What does it mean to you to be an 'imperfect, yet adored' child of God? How does this affect the way you look at others and treat them? How could it affect the way others look at and treat you?

Wednesday 21 June

1. Recall a time when you judged someone based on the way he or she looked or because you had a preconceived idea of how the person should behave. What was the situation? How did you respond to the person? What did you learn from the experience?

2. The writer says, 'I learned that it is not my place to judge but to help.' What do you think of this statement? Do you agree or disagree with it? Is this true in all situations?

3. Whose actions in this meditation do you more closely identify with— the husband or the wife? Why?

4. Have you ever had reservations about giving money to someone like the man in today's meditation? Why were you hesitant to give to the person?

5. How will you respond the next time someone asks you for money?

Wednesday 28 June

1. When have you held onto something that you couldn't seem to let go of? What prevented you from letting go of it?

2. Do you like to feel in control of your problems? Why or why not? What do we risk by fully turning our problems over to God? What could we gain?

3. What is your initial reaction to a problem that seems insurmountable? How has the way in which you react to a problem changed over the course of your life?

4. Can you think of any characters in scripture who turned their problems over to God? What was the outcome of their situations? What can we learn from them?

5. What problem can you let go of today? What positive effect could it have on your life to give this problem entirely to God?

Wednesday 5 July

1. When have you felt inspired to create something? Why were you inspired? What did you create? What did you do with your creation when it was complete?

2. Recall a time when you sensed God encouraging you to do something for someone else. How did you recognise God's voice in that moment? How did you respond?

3. Do you have friends or family members who are not Christians? If so, describe your relationship with them. What is challenging or frustrating about those relationships? How have those relationships surprised you or encouraged you?

4. Recall a time when you felt worthless or unable to contribute in a meaningful way. Who helped you to feel useful or valuable? What happened to help you overcome those feelings?

5. How does your church invite and encourage all people to be involved in the life of the community? Name some ways your church could be more inclusive and encouraging to those who do not often participate or feel useful.

Wednesday 12 July

1. Imagine you are someone who wants to make the world a better place, and you commit to one small action that will improve people's lives. What action would you commit yourself to? How would you get other people excited about your mission?

2. Describe a time when you experienced a mini-miracle. What made you aware of God in that moment? How did this experience affect the way you think about or understand God?

3. What is your favourite miracle story from the Bible? When do you first remember reading or hearing the story? How has that story shaped your faith?

4. What mini-miracles have happened in your church or community recently? What makes these events miraculous to you?

5. How might you show others that God cares about even the small moments of their lives?

Wednesday 19 July

1. What do you remember being fascinated by as a child? Why were you fascinated by it? Are you still interested in it, or did you outgrow your fascination?

2. How important to you is giving money as a way of living out your faith? Who or what has shaped your understanding of faith and money?

3. Are there particular causes, people or organisations you give money to? Why do you give to these particular organisations? How do their missions align with your faith?

4. Today's writer says, 'I believe that as citizens of the world we are called to make a difference with whatever we have and however we can.' Do you agree or disagree with this statement? How do you try to make a difference in your community or in the world?

5. How does your church participate in making a difference locally and globally? Name some other ways your church community could serve the world.

Wednesday 26 July

1. When you read the words, 'Do not fear' in the Bible, how do you respond? Are these words comforting? Frustrating? Challenging? Hopeful?

2. In today's meditation, Phyllis says she writes her concerns and worries in the margins of her Bible. How do you deal with your fears and worries? Do you document them? Do you pray about them? What helps you turn your worries over to God?

3. Describe a time when you felt overwhelmed by fear or worry. What did you pray about during that time? What happened? Did you feel that God answered your prayers? Why or why not?

4. When you are waiting for an answer to prayer or to see how a particular situation will unfold, what helps you to be patient? What prayers, Bible passages or activities help you to wait for God's timing?

5. What is the role of the church in praying and answering prayer? How does your church community pray for its members? How does your church acknowledge answers to prayer?

Wednesday 2 August

1. Recall a time when you or someone you know experienced a serious conflict with a family member. How long did the conflict last? What was the outcome of the situation?

2. Have you ever been asked to help two people settle an argument? If so, what was that experience like? What was most challenging for you? What ultimately helped the arguing parties move forward?

3. If you have not been the mediator of an argument, how might you try to help two people or groups resolve a conflict? What strategies would you use? What stories would you tell? What parts of scripture might help as you seek a resolution?

4. How does your church deal with disagreements or conflict? Who are the mediators in your church community? What do you admire about these people? How does their faith help them to be good mediators?

5. What helps you keep Christ at the centre of your life? What spiritual practices keep you focused on your faith? What new practice could you try to refocus your life on Christ?

Wednesday 9 August

1. Can you relate to Sharon's story in today's meditation? Describe a time when you wanted to attempt something new or challenging. What excited you about that challenge? What made you hesitate? What did you ultimately decide to do?

2. Who in your life has taken on challenges and succeeded? What do you admire about this person? What qualities do you share with this person? How are you different? What can you learn from him or her?

3. When you think about overcoming challenges, what character from the Bible comes to mind? How does this character or story help you to think about your own challenges differently?

4. In addition to reading scripture, how do you listen for God's direction? What practices or other resources help you to trust God in your daily life?

5. Who are the teachers in your community of faith? Who do you look to for spiritual wisdom and guidance? How do these teachers live out their faith?

Wednesday 16 August

1. What do you think of Claire's description of James as a 'hidden disciple'? What other hidden disciples can you think of from the Bible?

2. Are you or have you ever been a hidden disciple? Are you comfortable serving in the background or do you prefer to take a more public role?

3. What are some of the strengths of being a hidden disciple? What are some of the drawbacks?

4. Who are the hidden disciples in your church community? Do you know them by name? How do these disciples serve others? How does the community recognise or include these disciples in the life of the church?

5. What does it mean to you to be a follower of Jesus? What are some characteristics of a faithful disciple?

Wednesday 23 August

1. When people say they are 'working for the Lord', what do you imagine them doing? What does it mean to you to work for the Lord?

2. Do you feel that your daily tasks are part of your Christian service? Why or why not? What would make it easier for you to serve God in your daily life?

3. Name some ways you have served others in the past few weeks. Did you serve in these ways because of your faith or for another reason? How important to your faith is it for you to serve others?

4. Whitney says, 'We are called to serve with integrity and a positive attitude so that, whatever our occupation, we will bring glory to God.' Do you agree or disagree with this statement? What other words would you use to describe service to God?

5. In what ways does your church encourage people to serve? How could your church acknowledge and appreciate the talents and service of a wider range of people?

Wednesday 30 August

1. What was your first reaction to today's meditation? How do you relate to Maaraidzo's experience?

2. When have you been asked to represent another person or group of people? How did you feel about being a representative? What was the experience like? How were you received by others?

3. What makes someone a good representative? What characteristics, behaviour or skills would you want someone to have if they were going to represent you?

4. Who is the best ambassador for Christ that you know? What makes this person such a good ambassador? How do they practise their faith and share it with others?

5. Today's writer says, 'I am a good representative when I cease to live for myself and live for Christ.' What does it mean to you to cease to live for yourself? How will you live more for Christ today?

Journal page

Journal page

Thinking of You is a comprehensive introduction to the subject of dementia. This accessible book is a practical resource for those directly affected by the condition, their immediate family and carers, and those seeking to offer them pastoral care and encourage continuing spiritual growth. Importantly, the author addresses the spiritual care of the affected individual and how to help churches support them and their carers. The final section includes resources for ministry in residential care homes.

Thinking of You
A resource for the spiritual care of people with dementia
Joanna Collicutt
978 0 85746 491 0 £9.99
brfonline.org.uk

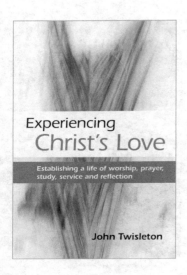

Experiencing
Christ's Love

Establishing a life of worship, prayer,
study, service and reflection

John Twisleton

In *Experiencing Christ's Love*, well-known writer John Twisleton reminds us of Jesus' gracious challenge to love God with heart, soul and mind, and to love our neighbour and ourselves. Against the backdrop of the message of God's unconditional love in Jesus Christ, the author delivers a wake-up call to the basic Christian patterns of worship, prayer, study, service and reflection. These, he claims, serve to take God's hand in ours, leading us into his divine possibilities.

Experiencing Christ's Love
Establishing a life of worship, prayer, study, service and reflection
John Twisleton
978 0 85746 517 7 £7.99
brfonline.org.uk

Jesus' parables intrigued, inspired, engaged and challenged the crowds, combining everyday imagery with surprising twists that prompted all ages to wonder and discover the treasures of the kingdom of heaven for themselves. Through 25 tried-and-tested retellings, together with sections on the importance of story, the power of parable and the challenge of all-age storytelling, this resource communicates the immediacy and relevance of Jesus' message for Messy congregations today.

Messy Parables
25 retellings for all ages
Martyn Payne
978 0 85746 550 4 £7.99
brfonline.org.uk

This unique and groundbreaking book is a summons to a subterranean spiritual adventure, an odyssey of the soul. If you let it, it will invigorate and inspire a search for something deeper in the spiritual life, and will link you with trusted spiritual guides to support you as you progress in a journey of discovery. *Journey to the Centre of the Soul* mines the rich seams of Christian spirituality, risks the depths, faces the darkness and makes astonishing, transformative discoveries.

Journey to the Centre of the Soul
A handbook for explorers
Andrew D. Mayes
978 0 85746 582 5 £8.99
brfonline.org.uk

How to encourage Bible reading in your church

BRF has been helping individuals connect with the Bible for over 90 years. We want to support churches as they seek to encourage church members into regular Bible reading.

Order a Bible reading resources pack
This pack is designed to give your church the tools to publicise our Bible reading notes. It includes:

- Sample Bible reading notes for your congregation to try.
- Publicity resources, including a poster.
- A church magazine feature about Bible reading notes.

The pack is free, but we welcome a £5 donation to cover the cost of postage. If you require a pack to be sent outside the UK or require a specific number of sample Bible reading notes, please contact us for postage costs. More information about what the current pack contains is available on our website.

How to order and find out more
- Visit **biblereadingnotes.org.uk/for-churches**.
- Telephone BRF on +44 (0)1865 319700 Mon–Fri 9.15–17.30.
- Write to us at BRF, 15 The Chambers, Vineyard, Abingdon OX14 3FE.

Keep informed about our latest initiatives
We are continuing to develop resources to help churches encourage people into regular Bible reading, wherever they are on their journey. Join our email list at **biblereadingnotes.org.uk/helpingchurches** to stay informed about the latest initiatives that your church could benefit from.

Introduce a friend to our notes
We can send information about our notes and current prices for you to pass on. Please contact us.

Subscriptions

The Upper Room is published in January, May and September.

Individual subscriptions
The subscription rate for orders for 4 or fewer copies includes postage and packing:
The Upper Room annual individual subscription   £16.50

Group subscriptions
Orders for 5 copies or more, sent to ONE address, are post free:
The Upper Room annual group subscription   £13.20

Please do not send payment with order for a group subscription. We will send an invoice with your first order.

Please note that the annual billing period for group subscriptions runs from 1 May to 30 April.

Copies of the notes may also be obtained from Christian bookshops.

Single copies of *The Upper Room* cost £4.40.

Prices valid until 30 April 2018.

Giant print version
The Upper Room is available in giant print for the visually impaired, from:

Torch Trust for the Blind
Torch House
Torch Way
Northampton Road
Market Harborough   Tel: +44 (0)1858 438260
LE16 9HL   **torchtrust.org**

THE UPPER ROOM: INDIVIDUAL/GIFT SUBSCRIPTION FORM

All our Bible reading notes can be ordered online by visiting biblereadingnotes.org.uk/subscriptions

☐ I would like to take out a subscription myself (complete your name and address details once)
☐ I would like to give a gift subscription (please provide both names and addresses)

Title .... First name/initials .... Surname ....

Address ....

.... Postcode ....

Telephone .... Email ....

Gift subscription name ....

Gift subscription address ....

.... Postcode ....

Gift message (20 words max. or include your own gift card):

....

....

Please send **The Upper Room** beginning with the September 2017 / January 2018 / May 2018 issue (delete as appropriate):

Annual individual subscription ☐ £16.50   Total enclosed £ ....

Please keep me informed about BRF's books and resources ☐ by email ☐ by post
Please keep me informed about the wider work of BRF ☐ by email ☐ by post

Method of payment

☐ Cheque (made payable to BRF) ☐ MasterCard / Visa

Card no. ☐☐☐☐ ☐☐☐☐ ☐☐☐☐ ☐☐☐☐

Valid from [M][M][Y][Y]   Expires [M][M][Y][Y]

Security code* ☐☐☐   *Last 3 digits on the reverse of the card
ESSENTIAL IN ORDER TO PROCESS THE PAYMENT

THE UPPER ROOM GROUP SUBSCRIPTION FORM

All our Bible reading notes can be ordered online by visiting bible readingnotes.org.uk/subscriptions

☐ Please send me .... copies of *The Upper Room* September 2017 / January 2018 / May 2018 issue (*delete as appropriate*)

Title .... First name/initials .... Surname ....

Address ....

.... Postcode ....

Telephone .... Email ....

Please do not send payment with this order. We will send an invoice with your first order.

Christian bookshops: All good Christian bookshops stock BRF publications. For your nearest stockist, please contact BRF.

Telephone: The BRF office is open Mon–Fri 9.15–17.30. To place your order, telephone +44 (0)1865 319700.

Online: brf.org.uk

☐ Please send me a Bible reading resources pack to encourage Bible reading in my church

Please return this form with the appropriate payment to:
BRF, 15 The Chambers, Vineyard, Abingdon OX14 3FE

To read our terms and find out about cancelling your order, please visit **brfonline.org.uk/terms**.

The Bible Reading Fellowship is a Registered Charity (233280)

UR0217

To order

Online: **brfonline.org.uk**
Telephone: +44 (0)1865 319700
Mon–Fri 9.15–17.30

Delivery times within the UK are normally
15 working days. Prices are correct at the time of
going to press but may change without prior notice.

Title	Price	Qty	Total
Thinking of You	9.99		
Experiencing Christ's Love	7.99		
Messy Parables	7.99		
Journey to the Centre of the Soul	8.99		

POSTAGE AND PACKING CHARGES			
Order value	UK	Europe	Rest of world
Under £7.00	£1.25	£3.00	£5.50
£7.00–£29.99	£2.29	£5.50	£10.00
£30.00 and over	FREE	Prices on request	

Total value of books	
Postage and packing	
Donation	
Total for this order	

**Please complete
in BLOCK CAPITALS**

Title .... First name/initials .... Surname ....

Address ....

.... Postcode ....

Acc. No. .... Telephone ....

Email ....

Please keep me informed about BRF's books and resources ❑ by email ❑ by post
Please keep me informed about the wider work of BRF ❑ by email ❑ by post

Method of payment

❑ Cheque (made payable to BRF)   ❑ MasterCard / Visa

Card no. ☐☐☐☐ ☐☐☐☐ ☐☐☐☐ ☐☐☐☐ ☐☐☐☐

Valid from ☐☐ ☐☐   Expires ☐☐ ☐☐   Security code* ☐☐☐
Last 3 digits on the reverse of the card

Signature* .... Date .... /......... /.........
*ESSENTIAL IN ORDER TO PROCESS YOUR ORDER

The Bible Reading Fellowship Gift Aid Declaration

giftaid it

Please treat as Gift Aid donations all qualifying gifts of money made
❑ today, ❑ in the past four years, ❑ and in the future **or** ❑ My donation does not qualify for Gift Aid.
I am a UK taxpayer and understand that if I pay less Income Tax and/or Capital Gains Tax in the current tax
year than the amount of Gift Aid claimed on all my donations, it is my responsibility to pay any difference.
Please notify BRF if you want to cancel this declaration, change your name or home address, or no longer
pay sufficient tax on your income and/or capital gains.

Please return this form to: BRF, 15 The Chambers, Vineyard, Abingdon OX14 3FE | enquiries@brf.org.uk
To read our terms and find out about cancelling your order, please visit **brfonline.org.uk/terms**.

The Bible Reading Fellowship (BRF) is a Registered Charity (233280)

This page is left blank for your notes.